BEYOND REASONABLE DOUBT

BEYOND
reasonable
DOUBT

G. H. Duggan, S.M.

St. Paul Books & Media

Imprimi potest:
    F. Bliss, S.M.
    Provincial, New Zealand

Imprimatur:
    Thomas Cardinal Williams
    Archbishop of Wellington

Library of Congress Cataloging-in-Publication Data

Duggan, G. H. 1912-
    Beyond reasonable doubt.

    1. Catholic Church—Apologetic works.   I. Title.
BX1752.D84   1987   230'.2   87-5457

ISBN 0-8198-3321-5 c
        0-8198-3322-3 p

1 2 3 4 5 6 7 8 9   95 94 93 92 91 90 89 88 87

Printed in the U.S.A., by the Daughters of St. Paul
50 St. Paul's Ave., Boston, MA 02130

The Daughters of St. Paul are an international congregation of women religious serving the Church with the communications media.

CONTENTS

VIII. The Primacy of the Roman Pontiff .. 187

Acknowledgments

The author records his thanks to the publishers of the following copyright works, from which he has made quotations:

Messrs. Burns & Oates, Ltd., for *The God of Reason* (R. Jolivet);

Cambridge University Press for *The Origin of Christology* (C. F. D. Moule);

Collins Publishers for *The Gospels and the Jesus of History* (Xavier Léon-Dufour), and for *The Resurrection of Jesus* (M. Ramsay);

Darton, Longman & Todd for *The Easter Jesus* (G. O'Collins);

Dominican Publications for *Philosophy for the Layman* (A. E. Doolan);

C. W. K. Gleerup for *Memory and Manuscript* (B. Gerhardsson);

Victor Gollancz Ltd., for *The Man Born To Be King* (Dorothy L. Sayers);

Hodder & Stoughton, Ltd., for *The Ring of Truth* (J. B. Phillips), and for *I Believe in the Resurrection of Jesus* (G. E. Ladd), and for *A Lawyer Among the Theologians* (Norman Anderson);

Macmillan & Company, Ltd., for *The Gospel According to St. Mark* (Vincent Taylor);

A. R. Mowbray & Company, Ltd., for *Jesus, Master and Lord* (H. E. W. Turner);

Our Sunday Visitor, Inc., for *The Eternal Son* (L. Bouyer);

Penguin Books, Ltd., for *Early Christian Writings* (tr. Maxwell Staniforth);

SCM Press, Ltd., and Charles Scribners Sons, Inc., for *New Testament Theology* (Joachim Jeremias);

SCM Press, Ltd., for *New Testament Theology* (Ethelbert Stauffer);

SCM Press, Ltd., and Westminster Press, Ltd., for *Redating the New Testament* (John A. T. Robinson), and for *The Gospels and Acts* (William Barclay), and for *The Christology of the New Testament* (Oscar Cullmann), and for *The Work and Words of Jesus* (A. M. Hunter);

Messrs. Sheed & Ward, Ltd., for *Jesus Christ* (L. De Grandmaison);

The Society for Promoting Christian Knowledge for *The Church and the Papacy* (T. G. Jalland).

Preface

Fifty years ago, the claim of the Catholic Church to be given a hearing at the bar of reason was being pressed by such stalwarts of the Faith as G. K. Chesterton, Arnold Lunn and Ronald Knox, and not a few people were influenced by their writings to examine the Church's claims and eventually to accept them.

In the last few decades, however, apologetics has been out of favor in Catholic circles. The simple proclamation of the Gospel message, combined with the example of a fervent Christian life, it was held, was all that was needed to lead people to accept the Faith. This position has been largely abandoned, but the suspicion of apologetics remains.

For this recent neglect of apologetics we have paid dearly, for there can be little doubt that if many of our young people have drifted away from the Church to join esoteric cults, this is due in some measure to the weakness of a catechesis which did not provide them with an account of the rational grounds for our beliefs in God, in Jesus Christ and in the Church He founded.

But it looks as if the tide is beginning to turn. In 1978, Christendom College published a collection of essays, entitled *Reasons for Hope,* to meet the need for some apologetics in college education in the U.S.A. and part of the cost of publication was met by donations from parents who wanted something of this kind for their sons and daughters. Then in 1981, *L'Osservatore Romano* carried an article "Apologia for Apologetics," which was a plea for the reinstatement of apologetics as a part of Catholic doctrine.

Beyond Reasonable Doubt is not an exhaustive account of the subject, but it does discuss the issues that are central to any account of Catholic, or indeed Christian apologetics.

On disputed issues, fashions change and the only pertinent question to be asked about a certain view is not whether it is fashionable, but whether it is true, or, where certainty is not attainable, whether it is probable.

The book has been written for the educated laity as well as for college and university students, and if it serves to convince any of its readers that there is more to be said for the reasonableness of the Catholic Faith than one would gather from some recent works, it will not have been written in vain.

I. The Nature and History of Apologetics

Apologetics, sometimes called Fundamental Theology, is that branch of Catholic theology which establishes the reasonableness of the act of faith. It is a comprehensive, systematic vindication of the grounds of Catholic belief and it has a threefold aim:

1. To strengthen the Faith of believers by showing that their acceptance of the Catholic Faith, far from requiring the abdication of their rational certitudes, is in full harmony with these certitudes;
2. To lead inquirers to recognize the reasonableness of the Christian revelation as this is expounded by the Catholic Church;
3. To refute the objections of those who reject this revelation.

The word *apologetics* is derived from the Greek word *apologia,* which means "a defense"; the form of the word indicates that it is an ordered body of knowledge like physics or ethics.

In developing his arguments the apologist employs philosophical and historical reasoning. Apologetics, however, is not a branch of philosophy or history, nor an intermediate discipline lying between philosophy and theology, but is an integral part of theology. The apologist is a theologian. Possessing the virtue of faith, he is guided by Sacred Scripture and Catholic Tradition in his choice of arguments and the way he develops them, as he shows that it is reasonable to believe that God has revealed Himself in Jesus Christ and that Christ established a Church to ensure that the truths He revealed would be taught without falsification until the end of time.

The relation between apologetics and Dogmatic Theology is similar to that which exists in philosophy between Epistemology and General Metaphysics. It is the function of Epistemology, or as it is sometimes called, Defensive Metaphysics, to show that idealism and scepticism, which deny that the human mind can know extra-mental reality with certainty, are false. This being established, it follows that General Metaphysics, which discusses the nature of extra-mental reality, is not a chimerical enterprise. In the same way, apologetics establishes the possibility of divine revelation by refuting Materialism, which denies the existence of God; Agnosticism, which holds that human reason cannot establish with certainty that God exists; and Rationalism, which holds that a supernatural revelation is impossible, or if it were possible, that it would be superfluous, since human reason by itself suffices for the right ordering of human life.

When apologetics has done its work, the dogmatic theologian, who is concerned with expounding the mysteries of the Christian Faith, can go about his business with equanimity.

The History of Apologetics

In the New Testament

Christian apologetics has a long and honorable history, beginning in New Testament times, for we find St. Peter making a plea for apologetical reasoning when he writes: "Always be prepared to make a defense *[apologia]* to anyone who calls you to account for the hope that is in you" (1 Pt. 3:15).

Our Lord Himself engaged in apologetical argument when He appealed to His miracles as proof that He was sent by the Father and possessed supernatural powers. His works, He said, bear witness that the Father had sent Him

(Jn. 5:36), and addressing the Apostle Philip, He appealed to His miracles as warrant for demanding faith in Him: "Do you not believe that I am in the Father and the Father in me?... Believe me that I am in the Father and the Father in me; or else believe me for the sake of the works themselves" (Jn. 14:10, 11). Earlier, in order to establish that He had the power to forgive sins, He miraculously cured a paralytic. Addressing the scribes, who were inwardly accusing Him of blasphemy, He said: "'That you may know that the Son of Man has authority on earth to forgive sins'—he said to the paralytic— 'I say to you, rise, take up your pallet and go home'" (Mk. 2:10-11).

It is clear from the opening verses of St Luke's Gospel that the evangelist in writing his Gospel had an apologetical purpose: "It seemed good to me...to write an orderly account for you, most excellent Theophilus, that you may know the truth concerning the things of which you have been informed" (1:3-4).

Indeed it has been argued that all the Gospels are apologetical in scope, being written for believers to show them their faith in Christ was well founded, and for Jews and pagans to lead them to faith in Christ.

In the Acts of the Apostles St. Luke has recorded only two of the sermons which St. Paul addressed to pagan hearers, and both are apologetical. At Lystra, the Apostle appeals to the witness which the visible creation bears to the existence of a provident Creator (14:14-16), and at Athens he argues that since men, who are the children of God, possess a spiritual nature, God must be a Spirit; as the Creator, who gives life and breath to all that lives, He must Himself be a living being, not an idol of gold or silver (17:23-29). Since the Jews were monotheists, there was no need to put before them arguments for the existence of the one true God. What they had to be persuaded of was that Jesus of Nazareth, who had been crucified on the orders of Pontius Pilate, was the long-awaited Messiah. Accordingly, the Christian apologetic directed to the Jews strove to show that the various Old Testament prophecies concerning the Messiah had been fulfilled in Christ. He

Himself laid the foundations of this line of argument when He instructed the disciples on the way to Emmaus: "Beginning with Moses and all the prophets, he interpreted to them in all the scriptures the things concerning himself" (Lk. 24:27).

The crucified Messiah, whom the Apostles were preaching, was so unlike the Messiah the Jews had been expecting, that we may be sure that there was a demand for credentials establishing the truth of the Apostolic message. These were provided, and they were of two kinds:

    (a) the witness of the Apostles who had been in the Lord's company during His public life, and

    (b) the witness of the Scriptures which had been fulfilled in Him.

We find both elements of proof in the authoritative tradition which St. Paul had received and which he handed on to the Corinthians (1 Cor. 15:3ff.).

It is very probable, as Gerhardsson has argued, that the Apostolic College in Jerusalem in the years after Pentecost devoted much time to searching the Scriptures for texts that threw light on the life, death and resurrection of the Savior. The fruits of this research would have been made available to the Christian preachers and teachers, and St. Matthew may well have drawn upon this store in writing his Gospel. It may also have furnished St. Paul with some of the arguments he used when he endeavored to lead his fellow countrymen to faith in Christ, as on that memorable day in Rome: "When they had appointed a day for him, they came to him at his lodging in great numbers. And he expounded the matter to them from morning till evening, testifying to the kingdom of God and trying to convince them about Jesus both from the law of Moses and from the prophets" (Acts 28:23).

Apologetics in the Early Centuries

From the time of Nero (d. 68), the Christian Faith was treated by the civil authorities as an unlawful religion, and the Christians were slandered by pagan propagandists as atheists who took part in cannibal feasts and indulged in sexual promiscuity. The apologists therefore faced a two-fold task—to refute the charge of atheism and immorality, and to appeal to the Roman Emperors, in the name of justice, for toleration for the Christian religion.

The oldest surviving work of Christian apologetics is the *Apology* which the Athenian philosopher *Aristides* addressed to the Emperor Hadrian in 125. Aristides begins with a brief account of the Gospel story and the spread of the Christian Faith, and then goes on to indicate the weaknesses of the other religions. The barbarians, he says, worship the blind forces of nature and lifeless idols; the Gods of the Greeks are notorious for their immorality, and the Egyptians, more stupid than the other nations, worship animals. The Jews worship the one true God, the Creator of heaven and earth, but they make too much of externals and they failed to recognize the Son of God when He came among them. That the Christians have found the truth is clear from the sublimity of their lives, for they are prayerful, charitable and pure, and they have no fear of death. "It is enough," he concludes, "for us to have informed Your Majesty, concerning the conduct and the truth of the Christians. For great indeed and wonderful is their doctrine to him who will search into it and reflect upon it. Verily, this is a new people, and there is something divine in the midst of them."

Some thirty years later *St. Justin Martyr* wrote two *Apologies* in Rome, the first about 150 and the second between 155 and 160. Both are primarily concerned with winning civil toleration for the Christians. The *First Apology* is addressed to the Emperor Antoninus Pius and argues that Christians should not be condemned just for being Christians. He describes their beliefs and practices to show that in these there is nothing deserving of death. The *Second Apology* is addressed to the Roman Senate and pleads for justice for the Christians. Christ, he declares, is the fullness of truth, and in His teaching will be found whatever there is of truth in the teachings of such men as Socrates and Plato.

In *A Dialogue with Trypho, A Jew,* Justin tells how

after studying the various philosophical systems, he was led to embrace the Christian Faith as the true philosophy. He then goes on to show that with the coming of Christ, the Law of Moses has been abrogated and that in Him the various Old Testament prophecies have been fulfilled.

In 177, *Athenagoras,* an Athenian philosopher, addressed *A Supplication for the Christians* to the Emperors Marcus Aurelius and Lucius Commodus, appealing to them as "conquerors of Armenia and Sarmatia, and more than all, philosophers." This plea for toleration, an able work and elegantly written, fell on deaf ears.

In the following decade *St. Irenaeus* published his great work *Against Heresies.* It consists of five works, the first two being devoted to the exposition and refutation of various Gnostic heresies prevalent at the time; the last three books contain a profound theological account of the Christian Faith.

The same decade saw the publication of the *True Doctrine,* in which *Celsus,* a pagan philosopher, attacked the supernatural character of Christianity. He denied that Christ worked miracles and the arguments he brought forward to show that the testimony of the Gospels is unreliable were echoed in the writings of the Rationalists of the 18th and 19th centuries. Celsus' book has been lost, but the text can be reconstructed from the detailed refutation which Origen published some seventy years later with the title *Against Celsus.*

In the *Epistle to Diognetus,* which probably dates from the second century, an unknown author begins by exposing the follies of paganism and castigating Jewish superstition, and then contrasts these with the sublimity of Christian revelation, drawing a singularly beautiful picture of the manner of life of the Christian communities of the day.

Clement of Alexandria (d. 214), who was head of the catechetical school of Alexandria, in his book *Protrepticus,* an exhortation to conversion, gives evidence of a knowledge of Greek culture that is wide and deep. Having himself experienced the appeal of Greek mythology, philosophy and the mystery cults, he is able to show how all that is of value in these is surpassingly fulfilled in Christ, the supreme Master of wisdom and Expounder of the mysteries.

All the works we have so far mentioned were written in Greek. Toward the end of the second century, works in Latin began to appear. Among these is the *Octavius* of *Minucius Felix,* a Roman lawyer who had been converted to Christianity. It is in the form of a dialogue in which one speaker, Caecilius, states the case for the pagan religion, and the other, Octavius, the case for Christianity, Minucius acting as chairman. The discussion is confined to such topics as the unity of God, Divine Providence and life after death, and there is no mention of the Christian mysteries of the Trinity, the Incarnation and the Redemption. The author was concerned only to remove the prejudices of the pagans and show how it was possible to take seriously the Christian claims. At the end of the dialogue Caecilius admits that he has been convinced by Octavius' arguments.

Tertullian, a Roman lawyer who was converted to the Christian Faith about the year 193, published his *Apology* in 197. In this work he proves with irresistible logic that the persecution of the Christians is completely opposed to the rules of Roman jurisprudence, for although the Christians were treated as criminals, the Emperor Trajan had ordered that they were not to be sought out by the civil authorities. After refuting the customary charges of atheism, promiscuity and infanticide, Tertullian goes on to describe in glowing terms the Christian way of life, a source of many blessings for the community at large.

In this book, *The Prescription of Heretics,* he argues that heretics are not entitled to a hearing, because Christ has entrusted His revelation to the Churches founded by the Apostles, not to these purveyors of new doctrines. Their appeal to the Scriptures should be dismissed out of hand, for the Scriptures belong to the Church alone. Early in the fourth century *Lactantius,* a rhetorician by profession, published a work in seven books, the *Divine Insti-*

tutes, in which he provided a systematic apology for Christianity. He points out the absurdities of the pagan myths and shows that there can be only one true God. He then argues for the divinity of Christ, appealing to His miracles and the fulfillment in Him of the Old Testament prophecies, and then goes on to provide an account of the Christian moral code. His work undoubtedly served to facilitate the conversion of many educated Romans to the Christian Faith.

Eusebius of Caesarea, the first great Church historian, writing in Greek about the same time as Lactantius, published a monumental two-part apologetical work, *The Preparation of the Gospel* and *The Proof of the Gospel.* The book seems to have been written in reply to a work by Porphyry, a disciple of the Neo-Platonist philosopher Plotinus, entitled *Against the Christians.* In the first part Eusebius refuted Porphyry's philosophical arguments, and in the second his historical arguments against the miracles and the resurrection of Christ.

St. Augustine was often engaged in apologetical argument with pagans and heretics. His greatest apologetical work is *The City of God,* written over many years and finished in 426. The pagans were contending that the calamities which had recently befallen the Roman Empire, such as the sack of Rome by Alaric in 410, were due to the abandonment of the pagan gods. To refute this charge, St. Augustine shows that the pagan religion was not the source of Rome's temporal prosperity, and is still less capable of bringing man to eternal blessedness; then he goes on to break new ground by providing a Christian interpretation of the history of the human race.

The Middle Ages

In the Middle Ages Christian apologists were concerned to meet the objections of Jews and Muslims and by reasoned argument convince them of the truth of the Christian Faith. There were Jewish groups in the West living by the Law of Moses and the Talmud. The Muslims controlled most of Spain and the coast of North Africa, and posed a constant threat to the Byzantine Empire.

In the East *St. John Damascene* published in 750 his *Discussion Between a Saracen and a Christian,* in which he put forward a reasoned case for Christianity.

Theodore Abu Qurrah, a disciple of John, in his book *God and the True Religion* shows that Christianity is superior to the other religions that claim to be divinely revealed—Zoroastrianism, the Samaritan religion, Judaism, Manicheism, Gnosticism and Islam—since it is better able to meet man's religious needs, and moreover is guaranteed by miracles.

St. Anselm (d. 1109) sought a more profound understanding of the truths of the Christian Faith and wrote not only for the instruction of his fellow-believers but also to refute the unbeliever.

The greatest apologetical work of this period is the *Summa Contra Gentiles* of *St. Thomas Aquinas.* It is said to have been written at the request of St. Raymond of Pennyafort to help missionaries working for the conversion of Muslims in Spain, but St. Thomas trains his sights on many targets, refuting not only the errors of the Parisian disciples of the Muslim philosopher Averroës, but various Christian heresies as well.

He begins by pointing out that the Christian revelation contains two kinds of truth. Some can be discovered by human reason using its natural resources, whereas others are beyond the range of reason and can be known only by divine revelation. In the first three books he deals with truths of the first kind, and in the fourth he discusses the articles of Faith which transcend reason, showing that although they transcend reason they do not contradict it. The doctrines of the heretics, on the other hand, contradict either truths known by reason or fundamental doctrines of the Christian Faith.

Modern Times

In the sixteenth century the Catholic apologist had to meet a new challenge, for he had now to defend the Catholic Faith against the attacks of the Protestant Reformers. Among the first in the field were *St. John Fisher,* with books refuting the errors of Luther and Oecolampadius, and *St. Thomas More,* who was engaged in controversy with Luther and various English heretics. They were followed by such men as Thomas Stapleton (d. 1598) and *St. Robert Bellarmine* (d. 1621). Bellarmine's great work *Disputations Concerning the Controversies of the Christian Faith* was an arsenal from which Catholic apologists were able to draw from the end of the sixteenth century onward. It was supplemented by the *Ecclesiastical Annals* of *Cardinal Baronius* (d. 1607), written to refute the Lutheran version of Church history put out thirty years earlier by the Centuriators of Magdeburg.

With the rise of Rationalism in the seventeenth century and its diffusion in the eighteenth, the central mysteries of the Christian Faith came under attack, and orthodox Protestants as well as Catholics sprang to their defense. *Blaise Pascal* (d. 1662) recognized the Rationalist threat quite early and planned a systematic work of apologetics. He died before he could write the book, but the material he had collected for the project, a series of disconnected but often profound reflections, was published under the title of *Pensées,* in an incomplete edition in 1670; the complete text appeared in a critical edition in 1844.

Pascal was followed in 1679 by *Huet,* Bishop of Avranches, with his massive work, *The Demonstration of the Gospel.* Two years later, Bossuet, Bishop of Meaux, published his *Discourse on Universal History* and he followed this in 1688 with his *History of the Variations of the Protestant Churches.* But these and similar works were unable to hold back the rising tide of Rationalism, and intellectual life on the continent in the eighteenth century was dominated by such anti-Christian thinkers as Bayle (d. 1706) and Voltaire (d. 1778).

In England *Joseph Butler,* who later became Bishop of Bristol and then Durham, published in 1736 a defense of Christianity against the Deists entitled *The Analogy of Religion, Natural and Revealed, to the Constitution and Course of Nature.* It was addressed to inquirers who, while conscious of order and regularity in nature, were unconvinced by the claim of the Christian religion that it has been revealed by God.

In 1794, *William Paley* published *A View of the Evidence of Christianity* which became a popular work of apologetics on account of its effective presentation of the facts in vigorous English prose. He followed this in 1802 with his *Natural Theology,* in which he developed at length the argument for the existence of God from the presence of design in nature. It is sometimes said that with the rise of Darwinism, Paley's argument is no longer valid, but as we shall see later this is not the case.

In his book *A Grammar of Assent,* published in 1870, *Cardinal Newman* discussed with great subtlety the process by means of which men arrive at certainty, and in the final section of the book he provides a powerful apologetical argument for the truth of the Christian religion. Throughout his adult life, he said in 1879, he had been engaged in defending the Christian Faith against the spirit of Liberalism, the doctrine that religion is not concerned with truth but is a matter of sentiment and taste.

Robert Boyle, the famous chemist who died in 1691, left funds for the establishment of a foundation for an annual series of lectures establishing the truth of the Christian religion against unbelievers of various kinds. The place of the *Boyle Lectures* has been taken by the *Bampton Lectures,* established by John Bampton (d. 1751). At first given annually, and now biennially, these have as their subject the defense and exposition of the Christian Faith, as expressed in the creeds, on the authority of Holy Scripture and the Fathers of the Church.

The *Gifford Lectures,* established by Lord Gifford (d. 1887), are delivered in the Scottish universities, and have as their theme questions of natural theology and the rational foundation of ethics.

In the early decades of the twentieth century the most eminent apologist for the Faith writing in English was *G. K. Chesterton* (d. 1936). In 1908, there appeared a brilliant defense of the Christian Faith against the errors of the day with the title *Orthodoxy.* In this book Chesterton took as the criterion of orthodoxy the Apostles' Creed. In *The Everlasting Man,* published in 1925, he argued for the uniqueness of man and the uniqueness of Christianity against the naturalistic evolutionism that inspired H. G. Well's *Outline of History.*

In more recent times the Christian Faith has been ably defended by *C. S. Lewis* (d. 1963). Refraining from debate on subjects on which orthodox Christians differed, he wrote—in defense of the central mysteries of the Christian religion—such works as *Miracles, The Abolition of Man,* and *Mere Christianity.*

E. L. Mascall, a priest of the Anglican communion, in his book *He Who Is,* published in 1943, provided a fresh account of the traditional arguments for the existence of God. In *Existence and Analogy,* published in 1949, he discussed our natural knowledge of God, and dealt with kindred topics in *The Openness of Being: Natural Theology Today,* containing the text of the Gifford Lectures for 1970-1971. In *The Secularization of Christianity,* published in 1965, he refuted the versions of the Christian Faith put forward by Paul van Buren in his book *The Secular Meaning of the Gospel* and by John A. T. Robinson in his book *Honest to God.* The final chapter, entitled "Fact and the Gospels," is a decisive refutation of Bultmannian scepticism regarding the historical worth of the New Testament documents.

Apologetics in the Teaching of the First Vatican Council (1869-1870)

The principles on which Catholic apologetics must be based were set out by the First Vatican Council in its dogmatic constitution *Concerning the Catholic Faith.*

Faith, as the Council defined it, is an assent of the intellect to *truth.* Faith, it declared, is "the supernatural virtue whereby, inspired and assisted by the grace of God, we believe that the things which God has revealed are *true,* and this not because the intrinsic truth of the things revealed is plainly perceived by the natural light of reason, but because of the authority of God Himself who reveals them, and who can neither be deceived nor deceive." This teaching was repeated and developed by the Second Vatican Council in its dogmatic constitution *On Divine Revelation.* In this document, faith is taken in the wider sense of "the faith that works through love" (Gal. 5:6), so that it includes not only its essential characteristic of an intellectual assent to truth, but also the commitment of the entire self to God. Since apologetics is concerned with establishing the reasonableness of the assent of faith, it considers faith under its aspect of an assent to truth.

A. What Is Truth?

Truth is a property of the intellect's act of judgment, the act by which we assert that something is or is not the case. A judgment is true when it is in conformity with reality, and false when it is not. Thus, if I assert that water is not an element, but a chemical compound, my judgment is true, because in fact water is a chemical compound. If, on the other hand, I assert that the whale is a fish, my judgment is false, because the whale, in fact, is not a fish, but a mammal.

We may distinguish between various kinds of truth, according to the subject matter with which the judgment is concerned.

Scientific truth is a property of judgments about the nature of things in the visible world, e.g., "The whale is a mammal"; "Water is composed of oxygen and hydrogen"; "The planets revolve around the sun."

Historical truth pertains to judgments about what has taken place in the course of human history, e.g., "Julius Caesar landed in Britain in 55 B.C."; "Napoleon was defeated at Waterloo in 1815 A.D."

Mathematical truth is a property of judgments regarding numbers or geometrical figures, e.g., "The square root of 64 is 8"; "Two sides of a triangle are together greater than the third side."

Moral truth is found in judgments regarding the way man is bound to behave in the exercise of his free will, e.g., "Man is morally obliged to worship God"; "Man is morally obliged to refrain from adultery."

Religious truth is found in judgments regarding God or creatures considered in their relation to God, e.g., "God is omnipotent"; "The universe was created by God."

The truths that most directly bear upon the right ordering of human life are religious and moral truths, for when we know these, we know where we come from, what is the goal of human life and how we must behave if we are to achieve it. Scientific truth is valuable as enriching the human mind, and providing us with the means of achieving temporal well-being, but it is of lower rank than moral and religious truths, since these are concerned with the ends of human life and its ultimate purposes, whereas scientific truth has to do with means.

There are, the First Vatican Council declared, two God-given means by which men may learn the religious and moral truths so necessary for the right ordering of human life: reason and faith. *Reason* is that which distinguishes man from the lower animals. It is because he has this capacity for abstract thought that he has been able to create science, philosophy, literature, political systems, religion and moral codes—of which there is no sign in the lower animals. The teaching of the Council on the role of reason in the attainment of religious truth is opposed to Fideism on the one hand and Rationalism on the other. *Fideism* is the view, espoused by Luther and others, that human reason by its natural powers is incapable of attaining any certain knowledge of religious truth, since our only source of certain knowledge in this field is faith.

Rationalism is the view, held by Spinoza, Kant and others, that human reason is all-sufficient. All that we can know—all that we need to know—about God and the management of human life is to be provided by human reason, rightly used.

Rejecting Fideism, the Council taught that human reason is capable of attaining some genuine knowledge of religious truths such as the existence of a transcendent Creator. But it also taught, contradicting the Rationalists, that divine revelation was necessary, and this on two grounds: first, in order that men might arrive quickly, with certainty, and without any admixture of error, at the knowledge of truths that were in principle attainable by unaided reason, and second, because man has a supernatural destiny, which he can know about and fulfill only by assenting to divine revelation.

When we assent to some statement, accepting it as true, we do so on the basis of *evidence,* which may be intrinsic or extrinsic.

Intrinsic evidence is the witness which the statement bears to its own truth, so that the human mind when it grasps the meaning of the statement sees by its own powers that the statement is true. Thus we have intrinsic evidence of the truth of the first principles of reason and of what we know by direct sense experience, e.g., the existence of the visible universe.

Extrinsic evidence is the testimony of reliable witnesses testifying to some truth of which they have intrinsic evidence. Such is the testimony of eye-witnesses in a murder trial.

When we assent to supernatural mysteries, such as the Trinity of Persons in God, of which we have no direct experience, our assent is based on extrinsic evidence. We accept this as the truth, not because we have seen it for ourselves, but because it has been revealed by God, who sees the realities of which He speaks: "No one has ever seen God; the only Son, who is in the bosom of the Father, he has made him known" (Jn. 1:18).

B. How Is God's Testimony Made Known to Us?

It seems that God could have chosen to communicate His revelation to each man individually, but this would not have been in accord with man's social nature and in fact His message comes to most men mediately, through the witness of other men. Under the Old Law, men received divine revelation from Moses, and after him, from priests and prophets. Under the New Law, men receive it from Christ, not directly, but through the mediation of the Apostles and their successors, to whom Christ has assigned the task of transmitting faithfully the truths that He revealed.

How can men know that the revelation communicated to them by other men comes from God? Primarily, by an interior illumination brought about by the action of God Himself. This is the gift of faith, of which St. Paul speaks: "For by grace you are saved through faith; and this is not your own doing, it is the gift of God" (Eph. 2:8; cf. Jn. 6:44; 2 Cor. 4:6). This teaching of the New Testament is summed up by the First Vatican Council when it declares that "the assent of faith is brought about by the grace of God, with which man freely cooperates."

However, the Council goes on to point out that the assent of faith, while it is essentially supernatural, is in harmony with the demands of human reason, for there are rational grounds, called the motives of credibility, which justify, though they do not compel, the assent of faith. These motives of credibility, distinct from the revelation itself, bear witness to its divine origin. Such are, the Council goes on to say, miracles and prophecies. Since it is only God who can by His wisdom and omnipotence work miracles and bring about the fulfillment of prophecies made long before the events that fulfill them, these point with certainty, in a way that all men can understand, to the fact of revelation, guaranteeing that it is from God. The Church herself, the Council adds, is an abiding witness to her divine origin, which alone accounts for her growth from humble beginnings, the eminent holiness of so many of her children, and her continuance in being, in the face of obstacles that would long since have destroyed any merely human institution.

C. The Relationship Between Reason and Faith

Since God is the author of both faith and human reason, and He cannot contradict Himself, there cannot be a real contradiction between the truths which He has revealed and truths established with certainty by human reason. If, therefore, someone maintains that there is such a contradiction, he has either misunderstood some articles of faith or mistaken what is merely a matter of opinion for a truth that has been established with certainty by reason. Thus the evolutionary origin of man, which as Teilhard and others have expounded it, is incompatible with the dogma of original sin, is not a fact established with certainty by science, but only a matter of opinion.

It is a matter of historical fact that the Christian Faith, by sustaining men's confidence in the power of human reason, has been a bulwark against scepticism in philosophy and created the intellectual climate that favored the rise of modern science.

And on the other hand, the theologian, seeking to arrive at a deeper understanding of the mysteries of Faith, has to make use of reason throughout the enterprise.

To establish what are called the preambles of Faith, such as the existence of God and the immortality of the human soul, the theologian must employ rational argument.

He must also employ rational argument in establishing the motives of credibility, showing that Christ fulfilled the Old Testament prophesies, worked miracles, and rose from the dead.

In striving to explore the supernatural mysteries and perceive their inter-connection, he must make use of philosophical principles, which are known by reason.

Finally, he must employ rational arguments to show that the difficulties urged against particular doctrines fail to prove that these contradict truths established by reason.

References

Aiken, Charles F., art. "Apologetics" in *Catholic Encyclopedia* 1, pp. 616ff.

Cahill, P. J., art. "Apologetics" in *New Catholic Encyclopedia* 1, pp. 669ff.

Dulles, Avery, S. J., *A History of Apologetics*, Hutchinson, London, 1971. (Inadequate on Catholic apologetics.)

Whitehead, A. N., *Science and the Modern World*.

II. The Immortality of the Human Soul

The Question

Every living body dies, and man is no exception. At death, the vital functions cease and the body disintegrates into the elements of which it is composed.

Is this for man the end of the story? Is this life which he now enjoys the only life the individual human being will ever experience? Or is he more durable? Is there within his mortal frame a source of life that cannot die?

Clearly, this is an important question, for how we answer it will determine our outlook on this present life and our behavior. This point is made by the author of the Book of Wisdom in the passage where he describes how the ungodly, convinced that when we die the spirit dissolves like empty air, conclude that life is for enjoyment: "Come, therefore, let us enjoy the good things that exist and make use of creation to the full as in youth. Let us crown ourselves with rosebuds before they wither. Let none of us fail to share in our revelry..." (2:6, 8-9). Pope John XXIII in his encyclical *Ad Petri Cathedram* has argued that if belief in a future life goes, this present life ceases to make sense: "The end of life," he wrote, "is not complete destruction, but rather an immortal life and a homeland that will endure forever. If this teaching, this hope so full of consolation, is stripped from the lives of men, then the whole reason for existence collapses" (nos. 21-22).

A. Preliminary Questions

Before we discuss the immortality of the human soul, we must establish that man has a soul, which is distinct from his various activities and differs in kind from that of the brute animals.

B. Man Has a Soul Because He Is a Living Body

The visible creation contains not only bodies that are devoid of life but also an immense variety of living bodies. On the one hand there are such things as rocks and pieces of iron; on the other, cabbages and palm trees, cats and elephants.

What is it that causes us to differentiate between living bodies and bodies that are devoid of life? We distinguish between the two groups because we perceive that living bodies are capable of a specific form of activity that is not found in non-living bodies. The living body perfects itself by means of its own activity, whereas bodies devoid of life cannot do this. Plants and animals can absorb food, grow and reproduce their kind, whereas objects like cars are incapable of doing any of these things. In a word, the living body, and the living body alone, is capable of *immanent action*. Immanent action is so called because it remains within the acting body, contributing to its well-being *(Manere in* = to remain within). Moreover, the living body is *one thing*. This is clear from the fact that all its parts cooperate to secure the well-being of the whole. Thus, in an animal the various systems (digestive, muscular, nervous, etc.) contribute *directly* to the well-being of the whole animal, and to their own well-being only indirectly insofar as they are a part of the whole animal.

Because the living body, although composed of different parts, is one thing, and is capable of actions of a distinctive kind, it must have within it a principle that accounts for its unity and its capacity for immanent action.

This principle, the principle of life in a living body, is called the *soul*. The soul is not to be thought of as a complete entity, distinct from the bodily organism and dwelling in it, but as part of the living organism. It is responsible for the fact that the organism is one living organism and not just a collection of complex molecules enclosed in some kind of a container.

Living bodies found on earth fall into three categories—plants, brute animals, and man. There are therefore three kinds of soul—vegetative, sensitive, and rational. The plant begins life as a seed, takes in food, grows and reproduces its kind. The brute animal is capable not only of the activities found in the plant, but it is also capable of sense knowledge and can strive actively to ward off danger and secure what is good for it by locomotive activity. Man is capable of the activities found in plants and animals, but he also possesses the power of acquiring intellectual knowledge and of directing his activity to ends he has freely chosen. By reason of his body he belongs to the animal kingdom, but because he is intelligent and has free will, he lives in a different world from that of the brute.

The Human Soul Belongs to the Order of Substance

The universe contains a great variety of things, and these things possess certain properties and perform actions of various kinds. The philosophical term for the thing is *substance* and the philosophical term for properties and actions is *accident*.

Existence in the full sense of the word belongs to the substance. Properties and actions are real, but their reality is secondary and derivative: they can exist and be understood only as modifications of the substance.

To illustrate the distinction between substance and accident, we may consider a running horse. The horse is real and the running is real, but obviously we have here two kinds of reality, for the horse can exist and is intelligible apart from the running, whereas the running cannot exist apart from the horse.

Since reality is intelligible only in terms of substance and accident, it is not surprising that the distinction between substance and accident is reflected in language: we use nouns to designate substances, and adjectives and participles to designate accidents.

The human soul, as we shall see later, is not a complete substance; nevertheless, it belongs to the order of substance and is not an accident or a collection of accidents.

That the human soul belongs to the order of substance is the verdict of consciousness, for we are conscious that through the manifold experiences that constitute our conscious life, we retain our personal identity.

Only if we admit this awareness of personal identity persisting through our conscious life can we give an intelligible account of *the fact of memory*. For, when we remember an action that we performed in the past, there is included in this act of remembering the consciousness that we who are now remembering are identical with the person who performed the action that is being remembered. So we say, "I remember that yesterday *I* did so and so." Without this awareness of the continuing identity of the substantial "I," it is impossible to give a coherent account of the fact of memory.

It is because each of us is certain that he is the same person from the beginning of his conscious life to the present moment that we know that we are responsible for all the deliberate deeds we have performed. It is on this basis that we regulate our conduct, and all sane men do the same. Without this basic assumption regarding personal identity, no legal system could work, nor could contracts be enforced. The view that there is no enduring substantial subject of consciousness is called *Phenomenalism*.

Hume (d. 1776) maintained that acts such as thinking, feeling, willing are the only realities in our mental life; what we call the soul is nothing more than the series or collection of these mental states.

Kant (d. 1804) held that the substantial "Ego," or as he called it, the "noumenal Ego" cannot be known by the speculative reason. It is a postulate, an idea that we employ to give unity to our conscious life, but whether there is an objective reality corresponding to it we cannot say.

For *John Stuart Mill* (d. 1873) the soul is nothing more than a series of mental states that is aware of itself as a series.

In the philosophy of *William James* (d. 1910) what the word "soul" stands for is the stream of consciousness.

Hume admitted that his theory faces insuperable difficulties and that he would have been able to overcome these difficulties if he could have admitted that our conscious states belong to a substantial subject. But, he said sadly, he could not adopt this solution because it was incompatible with his philosophical principles.

The difficulties with which Phenomenalism has to contend are indeed insuperable. In the first place, it is absurd to hold that there can be an act of seeing without someone that sees. Next, if our conscious life were nothing more than a succession of states of consciousness, each of these states would be self-contained and isolated from every other. If we say, with Mill, that the series of states knows itself as a series, we assume a unity that is not there, when we speak of the series as "itself." To speak of these states as a stream of consciousness suggests a continuity in what is discontinuous, for our conscious life is interrupted by sleep.

Phenomenalism, in whatever form it is proposed, cannot account for our awareness of substantial identity, and so may be dismissed as false.

The Human Soul Is Spiritual

The human soul is united to matter so as to form with it one living substance, but it is not itself material.

The objects of which we have direct experience are material, and therefore when we come to speak of a reality that is not material, we have to make use of negative terms. So when we say that the human soul is not material but spiritual, we mean that it has no dimensions, has no mass or color or shape, has no parts and occupies no space. It cannot be transformed into other things, and so, unlike material things, which are subject to decay, it has a permanent hold on existence.

Materialist thinkers, since they hold that only matter is real, deny that man has a spiritual soul. For them he is just a very complex organism, not essentially different from the brute animals.

In ancient times Democritus (d. 370) and Epicurus (d. 270) taught that man is no more than an agglomeration of atoms and ceases to exist when these are dispersed at death.

In modern times Materialism has been expounded by such thinkers as Hobbes (d. 1679), Holbach, Helvetius and Lamettrie, the last named, who died in 1751, being the author of a book with the title *Man, a Machine.* In the nineteenth century, Marx (d. 1883) provided a Materialistic account of man, in accordance with the principles of his philosophy of Dialectical materialism. Perhaps the most influential exponent of Materialism in recent times was the Darwinian biologist Ernest Haeckel (d. 1910). In his book *The Riddle of the Universe* he expounded a theory of Monistic Materialism, maintaining that the universe is a single material substance subject to evolutionary change, man being no more than a transitory phenomenon in this evolutionary process.

The evidence that our soul is spiritual is derived from a consideration of our intellectual activities. We find by introspection that in our act of intellectual knowledge the object known is represented by an *idea,* which is an immaterial likeness of the object which it represents.

That the idea or concept is immaterial is clear from the fact that it is abstract and universal. It is *abstract,* designating the essence of what it stands for, and prescinding from its particularizing notes. Thus the idea "man," which signifies "rational animal" signifies what man essentially is, irrespective of his color, age, size, personal qualities, or place of residence. It is because the concept or idea is abstract that it is *universal,* representing with equal clarity every member of the class to which it applies, however large that class may be.

A *material* likeness, on the other hand, is *concrete* and *singular.* Such is the *image* that is formed in the imagination. This represents an object with its individualizing features—its particular color, shape, etc. It is an image of *this* object present here and now to the imagination.

To perceive the difference between idea and image, we may compare the *idea of a tree* with the *image of a tree.* The idea of a tree—"a woody perennial plant, having a single main stem or trunk arising from the soil and having branches and foliage"—represents what is common to a great variety of species and to all the individuals within these species. The image of a tree, on the other hand, represents only this particular tree, whether the image be clear or blurred. The difference becomes particularly evident when we compare the image of a myriagon—a geometrical figure having ten thousand sides—with the idea of the same figure. The idea is precise, and the mind finds no difficulty in discussing its mathematical properties. On the other hand we cannot form a precise image of this figure or hold an attempted image in our consciousness for any length of time.

A second reason for holding that our intellectual knowledge is immaterial is that we form ideas of realities that are not material. Such things as logical sequence, moral goodness, property rights are known by the mind but cannot be represented by a material likeness.

Thirdly, the intellect can reflect upon its own act of knowledge, and it could not do this if it were a material faculty. A material faculty, such as the power of vision, reacts in response to an external stimulus. Consequently, it could perceive its own action only insofar as one part was aware of being acted on by another part. When the intellect reflects on its act of knowledge, it is at once both the knowing subject and object known, and this by all that it is. From this it follows that the intellect has no parts, or is immaterial.

The Intellect and the Brain

Since intellectual knowledge is immaterial, it cannot proceed from the bodily organism or an organic power such as the brain. The brain is indeed involved in the activities that precede and accompany the act of intellectual knowledge, but plays no part in that act itself. That the intellect is not wholly independent of the brain is clear from such facts as these:

(1) prolonged intellectual activity produces fatigue;

(2) if the brain cannot function properly because of an injury or degeneration, this affects the activity of the intellect and may even render it impossible;

(3) intellectual knowledge of an object is always accompanied by the presence of an image in the imagination, which may be a pictorial representation of the object or the image of a word;

(4) man is stimulated to intellectual activity by the impact of material things on his external senses.

Such facts as these indicate that the intellect depends *extrinsically* on the external senses for the images from which, as from raw material, it forms its ideas, but they do not prove that the intellect itself is a material faculty. What they do indicate is that the union of soul and body in man is more intimate than some philosophers have held.

To sum up our argument, we must hold that the human soul is spiritual because it has a cognitive power, the intellect, which is spiritual. A substance that was wholly material would be incapable of activities that transcend the material order, and intellectual knowledge is one of these.

The Brute Animals

Descartes (d. 1650) and his followers maintained that the brute animal is a mere machine, devoid of consciousness and feeling. That this view is false is clear from the fact that the brute animals have sense organs and a brain, and manifest feeling in their behavior.

At the other extreme is the view of those who hold that there is no essential difference between man and the brute animals. The Darwinian theory that man evolved from the apes favors this view, and novels like *Black Beauty* give it a certain attractiveness. The brute animal has a soul, since it is a living organism, but this soul is not spiritual, since the brute animal is devoid of intellect and free will.

The brute animal not only has sense knowledge and purely instinctual behavior, but is also capable of learning by means of the association of images. Thus the dolphin can be trained to do certain tricks by being rewarded with a fish when it does what is expected of it.

We cannot inspect the mind of the brute animal from the inside as we can our own, but we can infer what goes on there from our observation of the animal's behavior. The dog, as we see in sheep-dog trials, gives evidence of sagacity, but its behavior can be explained without attributing to it any abstract ideas. It is capable of perceiving concrete relationships, but gives no sign of having grasped what is meant by the general idea of "relationship."

Because the brute animal has no ideas, it cannot speak. It may make noises which resemble human speech, but it does not communicate by means of words, since words are conventional signs that stand for ideas. It can make sounds which are caused by an emotional state and, for example, serve as a warning to its associates, as with the crow acting as sentry for the flock. But it is not necessary to go beyond the level of sense knowledge to explain this phenomenon.

Finally, if we attribute intellectual knowledge to the brute animals, we shall have to admit that they rank as persons, with the same rights as human beings. So Kant is reported to have said: "When my horse says 'I,' I will doff my hat to it."

The Human Soul Is United with the Body So as To Form with It One Substance

Although the human soul is a substantial reality and is spiritual, it is not a complete substance, as Plato and Descartes taught.

For Plato (d. 347), man is constituted by the conjunction of two complete substances—the body and the soul. The soul comes from the other world and dwells in the body for a time. It has the task of governing the body, guiding it as a rider does his horse or the pilot his ship, until at death it regains its freedom and returns to the world from which it came.

For Descartes, the soul is a complete self-conscious thinking substance and the body a complete material substance—in fact, an elaborate machine. Hence the human being is a composite of two distinct and complete substances.

Aristotle (d. 322) rejected Plato's conception of man. For him, body and soul in man form a single substance, just as in a horse or a cabbage. Man is one substance, not two. Whether Aristotle regarded the individual human soul as immortal is a question on which scholars are divided. It seems more probable that he did not.

The Fathers of the Church took over many of Plato's philosophical ideas, and in particular his teaching that the soul survives the death of the composite human being, but they could not accept his view that the union of soul and body is an unnatural state, since, as Christians, they believed in the resurrection of the body, and it would be absurd to suppose that in raising the body to life God was restoring it to an unnatural state.

St. Thomas Aquinas (d. 1274), on the question of the relationship of soul and body in man, agreed with Aristotle in holding that man is a single substance. He pointed out that we attribute to one and the same subject activities which are purely spiritual such as thinking, and activities in which the body plays a part, such as vision. Reporting on the data of consciousness we say "I am thinking" and "I see."

He therefore drew the conclusion that the human soul, although it is spiritual, is the *substantial form* of the body. This means that it is man's intellective soul that is the reason why his body is a living body, just as the soul of the plant or the animal is the reason why it is a living body.

But since, as we have seen, the human soul is spiritual, it differs essentially from the soul of the plant or the brute animal. Because the activities of the plant and the brute animal are wholly material, we infer that in their case, the soul, the vital principle that makes the matter in them living matter, is simply a part of the material organism. In Thomistic terminology the soul of the plant or the brute animal is a *non-subsistent substantial form*. The human soul, on the other hand, is a *subsistent substantial form*. That is, it possesses existence in its own right and not simply as part of the human composite. That is why, when the human composite of soul and body dies, the human soul lives on.

The Human Soul Is Immortal

Personal immortality, that is, the continued existence of the individual human soul after death, has been denied by various philosophers and theologians.

The *Materialists* hold that at death man is simply transformed into a number of other material substances.

The *Phenomenalists* hold that there is no substantial soul and therefore conclude that when man's conscious activity ceases, nothing is left of the individual person except the matter of which the body is composed.

The *Sensists,* also called *Empiricists,* hold that all human knowledge is sense knowledge such as we find in the brute animals. They therefore contend that at death man ceases to be in the same way as a horse or a dog when it dies.

The *Averroists* (disciples of Averroës, an Arab philosopher who died in 1198) were groups of thinkers who flourished in the Middle Ages and again at the Renaissance.

They held that the intellectual activity of all men is caused by a single being, the Active Intellect. This being is immortal, but at death the individual human being wholly ceases to exist. This theory was condemned at the Fifth Lateran Council in 1513. The council declared that the rational soul of the individual human being, even though it is united to the body as its substantial form, is immortal.

The *Pantheists,* like Spinoza (d. 1677), hold that there is only one substance which exists externally and manifests itself in the vital activities of man. When these activities cease, the eternal substance continues to exist, but the human person as a distinct individual ceases to be.

Oscar Cullmann, a Protestant theologian, claims that the idea of the immortality of the soul is not biblical but Greek. He affirms the resurrection of the body but holds that between death and resurrection, the "inner man," if he continues to exist, will be in a condition similar to that of sleep. Other Protestant theologians like *Karl Barth* and *Paul Tillich* have also rejected the doctrine of the immortality of the soul as non-biblical. Others who admit the immortality of the soul hold that only the souls of the just are immortal, the others being annihilated.

The *Dutch Catechism* asserts that "the whole earthly man dies," but he lives on in the warmth and light which he has spread in his lifetime (p. 471). It goes on to say that there is no trace in the Bible of the idea of a disembodied spirit (p. 473).

There is indeed no place for a disembodied spirit in the philosophy of Existentialism, but the Book of Wisdom speaks of "the souls of the righteous" (3:1) and there is no suggestion that these souls are linked to any kind of body.

The Sacred Congregation for the Doctrine of the Faith set out the teaching of the Church on the next life in a letter entitled *Recentiores* which was published on May 17, 1979. There are seven points of doctrine, and number three reads: "The Church asserts the continued subsistence after death of a spiritual element which is endowed with consciousness and volition, so that the human 'ego' continues in existence though lacking its bodily component. To designate this element the Church uses the word 'soul,' which is consecrated by its use in Sacred Scripture and tradition...and she sees no valid reason for rejecting it."

Some Catholic thinkers, like Duns Scotus (d. 1308), have held that we cannot prove by reason that the human soul is immortal, so that for complete certainty regarding this truth we must have recourse to divine revelation. *St. Thomas Aquinas,* on the other hand, maintained that the immortality of the human soul can be proven conclusively by reason, as being the necessary consequence of its spiritual character.

The Proofs of Immortality

1. The Human Soul Is Immortal by Its Very Nature, Because It Is Spiritual

As we have seen, the abstract concept formed by the intellect is spiritual. If it were a material representation of the object, it could represent only one individual with its particularizing characteristics. But, being abstract, it represents what is common to an indefinite number of individuals. It is therefore not material, but spiritual.

Since the concept is spiritual, the intellect which forms it must also be spiritual and likewise the soul, of which the intellect is a power, must also be spiritual. And because it is spiritual, it does not cease to exist at death.

There are three ways in which a living being can cease to exist:

(a) by direct corruption;

(b) by indirect corruption;

(c) by annihilation.

Direct corruption is the destruction of a composite substance by its transformation into another substance or substances. Thus when a horse dies, it undergoes direct corruption, becoming a mass of inanimate substances.

Indirect corruption is the process whereby some part of a composite substance ceases to be through the corruption of the whole substance. So when a horse dies, its soul ceases to be by indirect corruption.

Annihilation or reduction to nothingness would result if the conserving action by which God maintains the being in question were to cease. The existence of the human soul cannot be terminated in any of these three ways.

It cannot cease to be by *direct corruption,* since only composite beings cease to exist in this way and the soul, being spiritual, is not composite.

It cannot cease to be by *indirect corruption,* because it possesses existence independently of the composite. Since it is spiritual it possesses existence in its own right, and not simply as part of the human composite. Therefore when man, the composite, dies, the soul continues to exist.

It cannot cease to be by *annihilation,* for if God were to cease conserving it in existence, He would be acting in a manner contrary to His wisdom. Since the human soul, being spiritual, has a natural tendency to exist forever, it must be kept in being forever by God, who, as a wise agent, must confer on creatures what they by their nature require of Him.

2. Man Has a Natural Desire To Live Forever

Whatever exists seeks to retain existence in a manner that is in accord with its nature.

If a being is endowed with knowledge, this tendency finds expression in a desire, which follows on the knowledge and corresponds to it. So the brute animal is moved by the desire for self-preservation to seek food and repel adversaries.

A being endowed with intellectual knowledge knows existence in an absolute way, not as conditioned by limitation to a particular time, and so it can form the concept of an existence that endures forever. From this knowledge there springs a spontaneous or natural desire for existence without end.

Since a desire of this kind cannot exist in vain, a being endowed with intellectual knowledge must be able to exist forever: and such is the human soul.

The principle on which this argument is based is that nature does nothing in vain. So if we find that an animal possesses a digestive system, we are entitled to infer that food must exist somewhere. In like manner, if we find that nature gives man a desire to exist always, this desire must be capable of fulfillment.

3. If the Moral Law Is To Have Adequate Sanctions, There Must Be a Future Life

Since the moral law is a true law, containing precepts and not just good advice or exhortation, it must possess adequate sanctions; otherwise it could be disregarded with impunity.

But the sanctions available in the present life are inadequate, for crime often goes unpunished. Nor is remorse of conscience an adequate sanction, because the worse a man is, the less he is troubled by remorse of conscience.

There must therefore be a future life, in which the sanctions of the moral law can be imposed.

This life must be unending, for if it came to an end, the fate of good and evil men would ultimately be identical; and this would imply that the distinction between good and evil is not absolute.

In his book *A Rumour of Angels* the sociologist Peter Berger develops this argument, which he calls the *argument from damnation*. Concerning certain dreadful crimes, he writes: "The condemnation does not seem to exhaust its intrinsic intention in terms of this world alone. Deeds that cry out to heaven also cry out for hell."

4. The Universal Testimony of Mankind

It is a fact, established by social anthropology, that the vast majority of men, of every race and culture, have believed in a future life, in which the virtuous are rewarded and the wicked punished. This is one facet of the universal phenomenon of religion.

Sir James Frazer, the eminent anthropologist, bears witness to the universality of this belief among primitive peoples. He writes: "It is impossible not to be struck by the strength, and perhaps we may say the universality of the natural belief in immortality among the savage races of mankind. With them, a life after death is not a matter of speculation or conjecture, or hope or fear; it is a practical certainty, which the individual as little dreams of doubting as he doubts the reality of his conscious existence." What Frazer says of the men of primitive cultures is also true of civilized men. The beliefs of the Egyptians are enshrined in the *Book of the Dead,* which tells how Osiris and the other gods weigh a man's good deeds and evil deeds in a balance and pronounce judgment on the departed spirit accordingly. If we may quote Frazer again, "The question whether our conscious personality survives after death has been answered by almost all races in the affirmative. On this point, sceptical or agnostic peoples are nearly if not wholly unknown."[1]

This universal conviction regarding the future life cannot be attributed to any of the usual causes of error. Not to the influence of evil passions or vice, for this would rather incline a person to disbelieve in a future life where evil is punished. Not to an illusory desire for immortality, for the future life is an object of fear as much as hope. Not to ignorance, prejudice or the influence of early education, for the belief will stand rational investigation and has been held by men of high intelligence.

The only sufficient reason for the almost universal acceptance of this truth is that it can be readily known by the human intellect. Reflecting on our intellectual activity, we come to perceive that we transcend the material universe, since, as Blaise Pascal pointed out, even if the universe were to crush us, we would be superior to it, for we would know what was going on and the universe would not.

In considering this matter, the primitive man is at least as well placed as the civilized man, for this is a question where scientific expertise counts for very little. Moreover, the civilized man in the modern world has so much to distract him that he may fail to give the question the attention it deserves.

Aware that we have something in us that transcends the material order, men have consistently drawn the conclusion that man's spirit lives on in another world. The images used to represent this future life were sometimes crude, e.g., "The Happy Hunting Ground" of the American Indian, but there was no doubt in their minds about the reality of the future life itself.

Reincarnation

The ancient Egyptians thought that as a punishment for sin the souls of men passed into the bodies of brute animals, and after expiating their faults there, were united once more to a human body. Similar notions were expounded by Pythagoras (d. 507) and his followers, and they are part of the creed of Buddhism and of the system of Theosophy expounded by Mme Blavatsky (d. 1891) and Annie Besant (d. 1933).

These theories of reincarnation are based on a false conception of the human soul, as if it were a complete substance merely dwelling in the body. The truth is that the soul is only a part of the complete being, and is essentially adapted to the body which it animates, so that it could not animate another body, either human or subhuman.

All such theories rob this present life of its seriousness, for they teach that however badly we use this present life, we will have an opportunity to do better in another life. They are the fruit of arbitrary speculation, with no evidence to support them. No one has any memory of a previous existence, nor is there any agreement among the exponents of reincarnation about the number of times reincarnation takes place or what is its ultimate outcome.

With no verifiable facts to go on, each is free to adopt whatever view suits his fancy.

The Immortality of the Soul and Biblical Anthropology

In the Bible man is portrayed as a single being and the human soul is not regarded as a complete entity distinct from the body.

From this fact some biblical scholars have concluded that there is no place in biblical thought for the idea of an immortal soul that survives the death of the individual human being.

However, there is no warrant in the biblical literature for this conclusion, because both the Old Testament and the New teach that some part of man survives death.

According to the Old Testament, the dead lived on in Sheol, the abode of the dead, and although little was known about Sheol, except that it was a depressing place, its existence was not called in question. It would be surprising, we might add, if the Jews did not pick up some ideas regarding the future life during their long sojourn in Egypt.

With the passage of time, Jewish thought regarding the after-life became clearer, and in the Book of Wisdom, written about 100 B.C., the doctrine of the immortality of the soul is clearly taught.

That the spirit of Samuel lived on after death is supposed in the story of Saul's consultation of the witch of Endor (1 Sm. 28:7-20); and there are passages in the Psalms (16[15]:9-10; 49[48]:17) which suggest that the psalmist looks forward to a life beyond the grave. In 2 Maccabees 12:43-45 the author tells us that Judas Maccabeus had sacrifices offered for the souls of those who had fallen in battle.

The teaching of the New Testament is quite clear, even though some scholars have been led by their philosophical or theological preoccupations to question this. Barth and Cullmann, accepting the view of Luther that philosophy has nothing to teach us in the religious field, reject the doctrine of the immortality of the soul on the ground that this conception, derived from Greek philosophy, is incompatible with biblical thought.

The biblical conception of man as a single being is indeed incompatible with the teaching of Plato and Descartes, but it is in full accord with the teaching of Aristotle and St. Thomas that in man, spiritual soul and material body are united so as to form one substance. In the New Testament the Greek word for *soul* is *psyche*. In some modern translations, such as the Jerusalem Bible and the Revised Standard Version, *psyche* in Matthew 16:26 is rendered "life," where the correct translation is "soul." Christ's promise to the penitent thief (Lk. 23:43) supposes that his spirit will live on after he is dead. Similarly when St. Paul speaks of being with Christ when he leaves this world (2 Cor. 5:6-8; Phil. 1:21-24), it is clear that he believes that his spirit will survive the death of the body and live on in the other world.

Note

1. Cited in A. E. Doolan, *Philosophy for the Layman,* Dominican Publications, Dublin, p. 165.

References

St. Thomas Aquinas, *Summa Theologiae* I, qq.75-76.
Summa contra Gentiles II, chs. 56, 82.
E. Gilson, *The Spirit of Medieval Philosophy* (The Gifford Lectures 1931-32 (Tr. A. H. C. Downes) Sheed and Ward, London, 1936. In chs. 9 and 10 Gilson throws into relief the originality of St. Thomas' anthropology.
R. P. Phillips, *Modern Thomistic Philosophy,* Burns and Oates, London, 1934. Vol. I; chs. 14-16 contain a systematic statement of the proofs of the substantiality, spirituality and immortality of the human soul.
C. Bittle, O.F.M. Cap., *The Whole Man,* Bruce, Milwaukee, 1945; chs. 19-23 contain another systematic account of the same topics.
A. E. Doolan, O.P., *Philosophy for the Layman,* Dominican Publications, Dublin, 1844. In chs. 37-40 there is a popular presentation of the arguments for the immortality of the soul.

F. J. Sheed, *God and the Human Condition,* Volume I, Sheed and
Ward, New York, 1966. Cf. especially ch. 3 on the nature of
spirit.

E. F. Sutcliffe, *The Old Testament and the Future Life,* Burns and
Oates, London, 1947, describes the evolution of Jewish
thought on this topic in Old Testaments times.

D. G. M. Jackson, *Reincarnation,* A.C.T.S., Sydney, N.S.W., 1978.
A brief account and refutation of the main theories of reincarnation.

III. The Existence of God

Is the visible universe self-contained, or does it depend on a being or beings distinct from itself?

Throughout history men have accepted the second of these alternatives. Acknowledging the existence of an invisible world on which this visible world depends, they have endeavored to make contact with it by various kinds of social worship: prayers, incantations, sacrifices. In every city of the ancient world there were temples, and in our own day men are still building churches, synagogues, mosques and temples. Even in states where atheism is the official creed, inculcated in the school and diffused by intensive propaganda, religion survives. We may therefore take it as a well-established anthropological fact that religion is a permanent feature of human life. Indeed Christopher Dawson has argued in his book *Progress and Religion* that religion is at the heart of every culture, primitive or civilized, accounting for the features that enable us to identify it as a distinct cultural entity.

Religion is an enduring element in the human situation. But is it an illusion? This was the view of Marx, who held that religion is a myth devised by the rich and powerful to keep the poor contented with their lot, and Freud dismissed religion as a mass neurosis. These and similar views have come to be widely accepted in our contemporary Western society, where the dominant philosophy is secular humanism—the view that human affairs can be successfully managed on merely human terms, without reference to any reality beyond the world. Impressed by the achievements of modern science and technology, which have enabled man to solve many of his problems, the secular humanist has come to believe that science will enable him to solve the rest. This is the mental climate which favors the growth of atheism, which no longer carries the stigma that was attached to it in earlier centuries.

The Meaning of the Question: Does God Exist?

The word *God* here stands for a Supreme Being, a First Uncaused Cause distinct from the universe, on whom the universe depends for its existence and intelligibility. We are concerned with God, not as He is portrayed in Judaeo-Christian revelation, but insofar as He can be known by human reason. In Pascal's phrase, we are dealing with the "God of the philosophers," not "the God of Abraham, Isaac and Jacob."

The existence in question is *real existence.* When we say that God really exists, we mean that He is not just an idea which enables us to establish order among the ideas with which our mind is stocked, but is a reality that exists independently of our knowledge of Him, comparable in this respect with things in the world around us, which we know, but which do not depend on us for their existence.

The Question Is a Philosophical, Not a Scientific Question

Modern science, by laying bare the secrets of nature, has given man an unprecedented mastery over the visible world and even over human life itself, and this has led some thinkers to suppose that it can answer all our questions. But it is clear that there are some questions which it cannot answer. It cannot, for example, tell us what is the purpose of human life or whether a course of action is morally right or wrong.

So it is with the question of the existence of God. This is a philosophical question, and indeed, it may be said to be *the* philosophical question. "At the root of all man's restlessness and all his philosophical speculations," Régis Jolivet wrote, "there is, I think, only one problem, *the problem of God*. Does God exist, and if He exists, what is His nature? There, surely, is the question of questions to which all others lead, and which it is impossible to escape. Not only is this so from the standpoint of philosophy, which inquires into first causes and first principles and cannot therefore abstract from the problem of God without denying its very purpose, but also from the more broadly human standpoint; our whole life is determined by the question. For the meaning we find in human existence must depend entirely on the solution we give to the problem of the existence and nature of God."[1]

The Question Is Not Purely Speculative

The existence of God is not a purely speculative question like the existence of a satellite of the planet Pluto or the existence of vertebrate animals in the Devonian strata. Our way of life will not be affected by the way in which science answers questions such as these. On the other hand, if God exists, a number of practical corollaries immediately follow. At once it is clear that the human mind is not at the apex of reality and the human will is not absolutely autonomous. Since a person could find this situation irksome, he could be led to decline to consider the arguments for the existence of God or minimize their cogency.

The Question Cannot Be Answered by the Logician

Logic is concerned with the relationships between ideas in the human mind. The arguments by which the existence of God is established will have to be in accordance with the rules of logical thought, but the subject of our inquiry is not our thoughts but the real world, the mysterious universe in which we find ourselves, and which we are seeking to understand. Is the universe the ultimate reality, requiring nothing beyond itself to account for it, or does it depend on some reality distinct from itself? This is the question, and what we most need if we are to find the answer, is not the expertise of the logician but a contemplative spirit. We are called upon to look steadily at the universe and reflect deeply on what we see.

The Question Cannot Be Answered by an Appeal to Religious or Aesthetic Experience

The feelings of awe or exhilaration which a person experiences when he is at prayer or listening to great music or contemplating a sublime landscape may give rise to a subjective conviction regarding the existence of God, but they cannot by themselves serve as the basis of an argument that is objectively valid. Since religious or aesthetic experience is essentially personal, any data coming from such a source is incommunicable. An argument, on the other hand, is addressed to the reasoning power of anyone who cares to examine it, and therefore must appeal to data that are within the reach of all.

The Answers

Atheism is the view that God does not exist. The Materialist, since he holds that matter is the only reality, is necessarily committed to atheism. *Pantheism,* which maintains that the universe itself is God, is really a form of atheism. Stoic philosophy was a form of materialist pantheism, but some of the Stoics, like Cleanthes in his famous *Hymn to Zeus* spoke of God as a transcendent, personal being who governs the world by His providence.

Agnosticism is the view that human reason is incapable of answering the question one way or the other. The term was coined by T. H. Huxley, an avowed disciple of Hume and Kant. Fideism, the view that the existence of God cannot be established by reason but is known only by faith, is a form of Agnosticism.

Theism is the view that God can be known by unaided human reason as a really existent being on whom the universe depends for its coming into being and its continuance in being. *Deism,* as expounded for example, by Voltaire, is a mitigated form of Theism, asserting that God exists, but denying that He has intervened in the course of human history.

Theism in Pre-Christian Thought

Socrates, reflecting on the visible universe, inferred that God exists as a Providence who is responsible for all those things in the world that cater to human needs.

Plato thought of God as the *Supreme Good,* from whom all the goodness in lesser beings is derived. He also spoke of a Demiurge, a Divine Artisan, who is responsible for the order in the universe, but never identified this being with the Supreme Good.

Aristotle thought of God as Supreme Intelligence, Subsistent Thought eternally engaged in the contemplation of His own reality.

These great thinkers arrived at the idea of a single Supreme Cause on whom the universe depends, but so far as we can see, none of them thought of God as a Creator who brought the universe into existence out of nothingness, so that it depends on Him for the totality of its being.

For the conception of God as a Creator who brought the universe into existence by an act of His will we are indebted to the Jews. But speaking generally, the Jews were satisfied with the knowledge of God given them by divine revelation and did not engage in philosophical speculation regarding the existence or the nature of God. However, there was in Alexandria a large Jewish colony which could not but come into contact with Greek philosophical thought and had no option but to attempt to come to terms with it.

The author of the Book of Wisdom, writing about 100 B.C., contrasts the wisdom that comes from God with the wisdom of the philosophers. Rejecting the various conceptions of the Deity that have been put forward by the pagan thinkers, he declares (ch. 13) that the one true God, the Creator of the universe, can be readily known by the natural light of reason.

Philo (d. 50 A.D.) endeavored to create a synthesis of biblical teaching and Greek philosophical thought, arguing that many of the views of the Greek philosophers were in harmony with the revelation contained in the Old Testament.

Theism in Christian Philosophy

St. Paul, in addressing pagans at Lystra (Acts 14) and Athens (Acts 17), pointed to the witness which the visible world bears to the existence of the one true God. In his Epistle to the Romans he stated the principle which has guided Christian philosophers ever since and was quoted by the First Vatican Council when it defined that God can be known with certainty by the natural light of reason. The Apostle wrote: "Ever since the creation of the world [God's] invisible nature, namely, his eternal power and deity, has been clearly perceived in the things that have been made" (1:20).

The *Apologists*, as we have seen, refuted the charge of atheism that was leveled against the Christians, and in doing so put forward rational arguments for the Christian belief in the one true God.

St. Augustine, seeking a philosophical system which he could make use of in developing his theology, adopted the Neo-Platonism of *Plotinus* (d. 270 A.D.), correcting it where it was in conflict with the teachings of the Christian Faith.

The starting point of his principal argument for the existence of God is the presence in the human mind of truths that are eternal, immutable and necessary, e.g., the truths of mathematics. The human mind itself cannot provide a sufficient basis for these truths, since it is bound by time and is contingent and mutable. They must therefore have their ultimate basis in a mind that is eternal, immutable and necessary, and the only mind with these qualities is the mind of God.

St. Augustine also appealed to the witness which the visible world bears to its Creator and to the universal belief of mankind, but in his philosophical case for the existence of God these are only subsidiary arguments.

St. Augustine's approach to the question of the existence of God was dominant in Christian thought until the 13th century when *St. Albert the Great* and *St. Thomas Aquinas* rejected the Neo-Platonist philosophy and adopted that of Aristotle. They maintained, with Aristotle, that the primary object of the human mind consists of things to be found in the material universe. Consequently, when they come to offer proofs of the existence of God, they start, not with eternal truths in the human mind, but with the really existent material things which we perceive with our senses.

In the later Middle Ages the worth of these proofs was contested and there was widespread scepticism regarding the possibility of establishing the existence of God by rational argument. Reacting against this scepticism, *Réné Descartes* (1596-1650) created his philosophical system and laid the foundations of modern philosophy.

Theism in Modern Philosophy

Descartes has been called "the father of modern philosophy," and with justice, for although philosophers since his time have differed widely on a host of philosophical questions, nearly all of them have accepted his fundamental principle regarding knowledge. This is the view that when we know, what we *directly* know is what is in the mind, that is, the *ideas* in which the objects of knowledge are represented.

Descartes and many of those who followed him put forward arguments to prove that God exists. But if one accepts Descartes' view that knowledge is the contemplation of ideas in the mind, one cannot prove that God exists. And in due course a philosopher came on the scene who pointed this out.

This was *David Hume* (1711-1776). Starting with Descartes' conception of knowledge, he drew the sceptical conclusion that the human mind cannot have certainty about any reality outside the mind, least of all about God.

Emmanuel Kant (1724-1804), reacting against the scepticism of Hume, endeavored to save the validity of scientific knowledge. But he also accepted Descartes' theory of knowledge and came to the conclusion that reality as it exists outside the mind, the "noumenon" as he called it, cannot be known by the speculative reason. God, he maintained, can be attained only by the practical reason, as the guarantor of the moral order.

Man, Kant argues, is aware of a "categorical imperative"—a command to do his duty; he is aware also that his happiness depends on his submission to this categorical imperative. But since in this life happiness does not always result from this submission, there must be a future life in which happiness is attainable; and since a future life is inconceivable unless God exists, God must exist.

Kant rejected as invalid the traditional arguments from contingency and purposiveness—the "cosmological" and "teleological" arguments, and his criticism of these arguments has been accepted by great numbers of educated men as definitive, absolving them from any further consideration of these arguments. But since his rejection of these arguments is, in the last analysis, only a corollary to his theory of knowledge, if this theory is erroneous, his criticism of the traditional argument falls to the ground. And as we shall see, Kant's theory of knowledge is erroneous.

The latest thinker to follow in the footsteps of Descartes is *Hans Küng*. In his book *Does God Exist?* Küng begins with the assumption that Descartes' theory of knowledge is correct, and ends, logically enough, with the conclusion that atheism and nihilism are irrefutable. If one accepts that God exists—this is not for Küng a matter of rational certainty, but of "fundamental trust"—one chooses to believe in God because the alternative is nihilism.

The Proofs of the Existence of God

Preliminary Considerations

When the First Vatican Council repudiated Kantian agnosticism and declared that God can be known with certainty by the natural light of human reason, it paid a compliment to the human mind. And although it was concerned only with our knowledge of God, implicitly it took a stand on the problem of knowledge by asserting that by our natural powers of knowledge we can attain with certainty to reality outside the mind.

There were philosophers in ancient times (e.g., Carneades, Pyrrho) who questioned the trustworthiness of our powers of knowledge, but preoccupation with the problem of knowledge is distinctive of modern philosophy. This is a consequence of the almost universal acceptance of Descartes' subjectivist account of knowledge.

The fundamental question regarding knowledge is: What is the *direct* object of the act of knowledge?

This marks the parting of the ways in philosophy, with Subjectivism on the one hand and Natural Realism on the other.

Subjectivism is the view that the direct object of the act of knowledge is a *representation* of the object known.

For *Natural Realism,* the view of Aristotle, Saint Thomas and their followers, the direct object of the act of knowledge is not the representation, but the *object itself,* apprehended, whether by sense or intellect, as distinct from the knower. These philosophers agree that the knower is aware of his act of knowledge and can reflect on the image or idea in which the object is represented, but they deny that either the act of knowledge or the representation is what is *directly* known. When we know something, we do indeed know that we know, but we can do this only because in the first place we know something other than ourselves.

Subjectivism is found in two forms:
(a) *Sensism* or *Empiricism,* which is the view that all our knowledge is essentially sense-knowledge;
(b) *Conceptualism* or *Idealism,* which is the view that we possess abstract ideas distinct from sense-images, but whether it be image or idea, what is directly known is the representation of the object known.

Because Subjectivism, and its daughter, Scepticism, destroy the possibility of establishing by reason that God exists, we must clear the ground by offering a brief refutation of these theories.

Subjectivism Is False

In the first place, it contradicts the immediate testimony of consciousness, viz., that knowledge is primarily knowledge of some object distinct from the knower. In the act of knowledge we perceive the act itself, but only secondarily and obliquely, and our knowledge of the representation of the object known is similarly indirect.

Secondly, Subjectivism leads inevitably to Scepticism, for this account of knowledge leaves us with no means of determining whether the representation corresponds with the reality it purports to represent. For more than three centuries Decartes and his followers have been trying to build a bridge between the mind and external reality. They have not succeeded because it is impossible, with a Subjectivist account of knowledge, to bridge the gap.

Subjectivism in its Sensist form is false because it denies that we possess abstract ideas, reducing all our knowledge to sense images. *Scepticism,* which is the inevitable consequence of Subjectivism, is the view that, since the external senses and the intellect are unreliable, certainty about external reality is out of the question. This theory cannot be refuted directly, but only indirectly, by the proof known as the *reduction ad absurdum.*

It cannot be refuted directly, because this refutation would involve the use of the intellect and the sceptic has questioned its reliability.

We can show, however, that the sceptic cannot make a statement without contradicting himself and thereby committing himself to a position that is absurd.

On the one hand the Sceptic holds that there are no certain truths. On the other hand he cannot make a statement without admitting that the principle of contradiction is certainly true. According to this principle, being and non-being are not identical. If it is rejected, then in any statement "is" and "is not" will be interchangeable. It is obvious that on these terms thought and discourse become impossible.

The sceptical view that the external senses are unreliable can be maintained only if one holds that the external senses are not powers of knowledge but have some other function. For if one holds that the external senses are powers of knowledge, one must hold that they are essentially reliable. If they were unreliable, they would not be powers of knowledge, since they would provide unreliable information; and unreliable information is not knowledge.

A Note on Proof

Some thinkers, e.g., Mortimer Adler in his book *How To Think about God,* would restrict the term "proof" to mathematics and natural science. But this restriction is unwarranted. An argument is entitled to be called a proof when it establishes the truth of a conclusion by showing that it follows necessarily from premises that are true.

As will be seen, the proofs that God exists establish this truth from two premises, one concerning some aspect of the visible universe, the other invoking the principle of causality, which, because it is self-evident, stands in no need of proof.

Is It Necessary To Prove That God Exists?

There have been philosophers, called *Ontologists,* who maintained that it is not necessary to prove that God exists, because the first act of the human intellect is an intuition of the being of God. This view is contrary to experience. The first concept we form is that of being, but this represents being in general and it does not give us an intuitive knowledge of God. If the mind had an intuitive knowledge of God, as the Ontologists say, it would by its natural powers possess the beatific vision. The Ontologists could not say this, and they made such distinctions in the divine reality apprehended in the first act of the intellect, that there no longer remained a direct intuition of God. Their mistake was to take for an immediate intuition of the intellect a truth they had learned in early childhood and which so illuminated their interior experience that they had ceased to be aware of how it had originated.

Can the Existence of God Be Proven by the Ontological Argument?

The argument commonly known as the Ontological Argument seeks to establish that God exists from a consideration of what is meant by the term "God." It was first put forward by St. Anselm (d. 1106), and was adopted and expounded, with variations, by Descartes, Leibniz (d. 1716) and others.

St. Anselm argued thus:

"God is by definition that being than which no greater can be conceived. But if God did not really exist, it would be possible to conceive of a greater being, namely one that does really exist. Since the conclusion is absurd, the hypothesis that God does not really exist must also be absurd.

"Therefore God must really exist."

St. Thomas rejected this argument as invalid:

(a) because not everyone would be prepared to accept St. Anselm's definition of God; and

(b) because, if the definition is accepted, we cannot infer from it that God exists as a reality distinct from the mind, but only that He exists as an object of thought in the mind *(S. T.* I, q.2., a.1 ad 2um).

In other words, St. Anselm's "Ontological Argument" contains an illegitimate passage from an idea in the mind to reality as it exists outside the mind. The argument is invalid because our ideas of things express only the essence of things and do not include the note of real existence, and this is as true of our idea of God as of any other.

Kant, in his *Critique of Pure Reason,* rejects the Ontological Argument for the same reason, pointing out that the idea of a hundred silver coins is the same, whether we have the money in our pocket or our pocket is empty.

Descartes argued from the idea of God as "the infinite being" and Leibniz from the idea of "the necessary being," but both arguments suffer from the same flaw as St. Anselm's. For the existence implied in these ideas is *existence as represented in the idea,* not *existence as actually possessed in the real world.* From the contemplation of an idea we are not entitled to infer the real existence of what it represents.

If we are to prove that God really exists, we must start with the realities of whose existence we have direct experience, namely the things in the world which we perceive with our senses. These are the starting-point from which the human mind can, by using the first principles that are the natural light of reason, come to some knowledge of God, the Creator of the visible universe.

The Thomistic Proofs

A. Presuppositions

The arguments by which St. Thomas establishes the existence of God presuppose a number of truths that are established elsewhere in his philosophy:

1. The human mind can by its native powers acquire a number of certitudes regarding the visible universe, viz., that it exists as a reality independent of the human mind, that it is subject to change, consists of a multitude of beings, and that this multitude of beings constitutes a cosmos, an ordered universe.

2. The primary object of the human intellect, i.e., that which it first knows, is being, and the being that is immediately evident to the mind is actually existing material substances. In the concrete datum of sense experience, the

intellect apprehends the actual existent thing as existent, that is, as actually exercising that which primarily makes it real—the "act" of existence.

3. *The Principle of Sufficient Reason.*

Being has certain necessary properties and the one that concerns us here is that it is intelligible, i.e., capable of satisfying the intellect in its quest for understanding. Sartre indeed maintained that being is absurd, but this was merely a deduction from his postulate that God does not exist. If being were absurd, as he holds, then philosophy and indeed all rational thought, would be a waste of time.

4. *The Principle of Efficient Causality.*

This principle has been expressed in various ways, but the most exact formulation is: "Every being which has not within itself the reason for its possession of existence, must have this reason in another, namely its efficient cause—the cause which by its action brought it into being."

A being which has not within itself the reason for its possession of existence is said to be *contingent*—it happens (Latin: *contingit)* to possess existence.

If a being that previously did not exist comes into existence, it is obviously contingent: it happens to exist, but could as well be non-existent. Its possession of existence is intelligible only if it was brought into being by another being, its efficient cause. Hume maintained that it is possible to *imagine* that something begins to be of itself, independently of any efficient cause.

We may be able to *imagine* this happening, but, as Kant pointed out, we cannot *think* it. The mind, he said, is so constructed that if we witness some phenomenon we cannot but conclude that it must be due to some efficient cause. But in his philosophy, the principle of causality is only a *law of thought.* Whether the principle applies in the real world we cannot say, because the real world, the world as it exists outside the mind, is unknowable.

For St. Thomas the principle of causality is a *law of being,* expressing what must be the case in the real world. In other words, it is not merely a logical principle to which our thinking must conform, but an ontological principle that applies to beings as they are in themselves.

5. *The Principle of Limited Regress.*

This principle may be formulated thus: "An endless series of essentially subordinate causes is impossible."

A series of essentially subordinate causes is one in which each cause depends for its exercise of causation on the influx of causative power from the cause that precedes it in the series. An example of such causation would be that which is exercised by one car in a train on the car behind it, for it depends in its turn on the causative influence of the car in front of it. However long the series of cars extends, there would be no movement unless there were an engine at the head of the train.

A series of essentially subordinate causes is distinguished from one in which the causes are only accidentally subordinate, e.g., the successive generations of animals belonging to one species. These merely precede one another in time, and the later members of the series do not depend on the earlier ones in their actual exercise of causation, because they have a causal power of their own.

Essentially subordinate causes have no causal power of their own, so that, however far the causal series is extended, their exercise of causation is unintelligible unless it is derived from a cause that has causal power of itself.

B. The "Five Ways"

In his *Summa Theologiae* (I., q.2, a.3) St. Thomas sets out five ways by which the human mind, using its natural resources, can come to know with certainty that God exists. He calls them "ways" or "roads," indicating that they are, as it were, paths by which the mind may travel to the shore of the infinite ocean of being that is God.

Each "way" begins with some aspect of material things, and by applying the principles of limited regress and efficient causality shows that it can be adequately explained only if it derives its reality ultimately from God, the First Cause of the universe.

Taking in turn the following features of the universe, he argues thus:

(a) As composed of beings that undergo change, it must depend on an unchanging cause of change.

(b) As composed of beings which exercise causation dependently on causes distinct from themselves, it must depend on a cause that is independent in its exercise of causation.

(c) As composed of beings that possess existence contingently, it must depend on a being that possesses existence of necessity.

(d) As composed of beings that are limited in perfection, it must depend on a being that is unlimited in perfection.

(e) As composed of beings that are ordered to an end, it must depend on an intelligent cause who is not ordered to an end, but is an end unto himself.

We shall set out three proofs based on a consideration of the visible universe, adding a fourth based on a consideration of the moral order. The aspects of the universe with which we shall concern ourselves are its contingency, its manifoldness and its order.

C. The Proof from the Contingency of the Universe

This is a development of the "Third Way" of St. Thomas, and unlike the "First Way" and the "Second Way," which start with the phenomenon of accidental change, this has as its starting-point the fact of substantial change. It may be set out thus:

The material universe is a vast assemblage of beings, each of which is contingent, that is, it exists in such a way that its non-existence is a possibility. That such things are contingent is clear from the fact that they begin to be and cease to be.

An assemblage of beings, each of which is contingent, must itself be contingent, for its metaphysical status must be of the same order as that of its components, just as a carpet consisting wholly of green strands must itself be green.

What exists contingently cannot by itself provide an adequate explanation of its possession of existence. Being contingent, it could as well not be as be. If in fact it does exist, it must owe its existence to some cause that brought it into existence. If this cause is itself contingent, it must owe its existence to another, and even if this series of contingent causes is prolonged indefinitely, it cannot by itself account for its possession of existence.

Therefore we must come ultimately to a necessary being, that is a being who requires no other being to account for his possession of existence, since he has it of himself; and such a being is what we mean by God.

Note:

1. Mortimer Adler maintains that to argue from the contingency of all the beings in the universe to the contingency of the universe itself involves one in the fallacy of composition. But, as we have pointed out, the inference is legitimate since the agglomeration of individual substances that form a universe does not alter the character of these substances, whether they be elementary particles or compounds formed of these.

2. Mortimer Adler considers that the argument from contingency is the only valid argument for the existence of God. The cosmos, as a whole, he points out, is radically contingent, since it is only one of a number of possible universes that could have existed, and so it might not have existed at all. Such a universe needs an efficient cause to keep it in being, and such a cause must either be a necessary being or depend on some necessary being.

3. If any being exists, necessary being must exist, for the hypothesis that all reality is contingent is absurd. So the question about the existence of God is really a question about the nature of the universe, viz., is the universe necessary being or not?

   For the Pantheist, who identifies the universe with God, the universe must be necessary being.

But if he is logical, he will have to deny the reality of change in the universe, since necessary being cannot be other than it is.

4. The contingency of the universe is yet more evident if, as the Christian Faith teaches, it came into existence a measurable time ago, but it would be no less contingent if, as Aristotle thought, it were eternal. Many modern astronomers are of the opinion that the universe in which we find ourselves came into being between 10 and 20 billion years ago, but they refrain from speculating about the state of affairs before that date (cf. R. Jastrow, *God and the Astronomers*).

5. Leibniz expressed our insight into the contingent nature of the universe when he pointed out that it is not nonsensical to ask: "Why is there something rather than nothing?"

D. Proof from the Multiplicity of Beings in the Universe

This proof, which proceeds from the Many to the One, can be developed in a variety of ways.

Plato in his dialogue *The Symposium* pointed out that the presence of varying levels of beauty in the universe is intelligible only if these things, in which beauty is found in a limited degree, are dependent on a being that is Beauty Itself, Beauty pure and simple, without limit.

In his *Summa Theologiae* St. Thomas in his "Fourth Way" argues from the existence of degrees of perfection in things to the existence of a being that is supremely perfect.

In his work *De Potentia* (QQ. DD. 111, 5), St. Thomas argues that what is manifold is ultimately intelligible only as depending on the One. This is the form of the argument which we have chosen and it may be set out thus:

It is evident that there are many beings in the universe and that all of these resemble one another in this most fundamental characteristic, that each is *a being*.

But when two things which are not identical resemble each other in some respect, this resemblance must have some cause distinct from the things themselves. (This is the principle on which the evolutionary argument from homology is based—the argument that the similarity in the structure of the forelimb of mammals is to be accounted for by their descent from a common ancestor. The evolutionary conclusion may be debatable but the principle—that this resemblance must have some cause distinct from the mammals themselves—is sound.)

Therefore the radical similarity in beings which consists in this—that each is a being—must have some cause distinct from the things themselves, and this can only be a cause who is Being Itself and who by conferring being on each one is the cause of their similarity to one another.

E. Proof from the Order in the Universe

This proof, which from the existence of order in the universe, infers the existence of an intelligent cause responsible for this order, is called the *teleological proof.*

It was first developed by the Greek philosopher Anaxagoras (d. 428 B.C.), and it has been formulated in various ways since his day. Kant did not admit that it is valid, but he spoke of it with respect, and it is the proof that most people find easiest to follow. The proof may be set out thus:

We find in the universe, in things that are devoid of intelligence, an ordering of means to predetermined ends. But the ordering of means to predetermined ends requires an intelligent cause to account for it.

This cause is not to be found in the things themselves, since they lack intelligence: it must therefore exist apart from them.

If this intelligent cause is ordained to an end distinct from itself, the ordering will have to be done by another intelligent cause, and since such a series of causes cannot be prolonged indefinitely, we must come ultimately to an intelligent cause who is an end unto Himself because He is

Supreme Goodness itself: and such a being is what we mean by the term "God."

Elucidations:

1. The ordering of means to predetermined ends is most clearly seen in living bodies, e.g., the structure of the human eye, which is similar to that of a camera; the organization of proteins in the living cell; the compartments in the abdomen of the bombardier beetle. But this order is a characteristic of all natural bodies, whether living or non-living, since each one exists in order that by its actions it may achieve its appropriate end. Thus water exists in order that it may fulfill its role in the universe, e.g., by contributing to the maintenance of life.

The visible universe is a universe of natures which behave in regular fashion in accordance with certain laws. These laws are embodied in the things themselves, being constituted by the orientation of the things to their respective ends and to the actions by which these ends are to be achieved.

Besides the orientation of individual things to their particular ends, which is called *intrinsic finality,* there is also the coordination of several agents to the attainment of a common end, e.g., the mutual adaptation of plants and animals to secure the balance of nature; this coordination is called *extrinsic finality.*

2. The existence of order requires an intelligent cause to account for it because the end, which does not exist in physical reality, determines the means by which it is to be achieved. It cannot exercise causality unless it exists in some way. But it does not exist in physical reality. It must therefore exist in the only other way possible to it, that is, as an idea or plan in the mind of an intelligent cause.

Consider, for example, the structure of the eye in a human fetus. This structure is determined by the act of vision to which it is ordained, even though this act has not yet taken place. Vision being the kind of action it is, the eye must have the structure required to bring it about.

William Paley, in his *Natural Theology,* published in

1802, argued that, just as we infer the existence of a human artificer from the design evident in the products of human ingenuity such as a watch, so we may infer *a fortiori* the existence of a superhuman designer from the evidence of design in natural objects such as living organisms. Paley's argument, as far as it goes, is valid, and contrary to the popular view, it was not refuted by Charles Darwin. In his book, *The Origin of Species,* published in 1859, Darwin argued that the structures which Paley took for evidence of design could be accounted for by the natural selection of chance variations. In attributing the formation of organic structures such as the human eye to chance, Darwin aligned himself with such ancient philosophers as Empedocles (d. 430), Democritus (d. 360) and Epicurus (d. 270).

Empedocles maintained that the arrangement of the teeth in the jaw, with incisors in the front and molars at the back, was due to chance; the animal which by chance found itself with this arrangement survived, and the others with less suitable arrangements perished.

Aristotle deals with Empedocles' theory in his *Physics* (Bk. 2, ch. 6), where he points out that even if the arrangement of the teeth came about as Empedocles had suggested, his theory could not account for the fact that the same arrangement persisted in subsequent generations

Darwin's theory suffers from the same fatal weakness. Devised with the object of eliminating true purposiveness from nature, it incorporates two factors which imply true purposiveness. These are the struggle for existence and heredity—the tendency of the organism to strive to preserve its life, and the tendency to perpetuate the species by handing on its characteristics to its offspring. These two tendencies are intelligible only if the activity of the organism is oriented to a predetermined end. And this implies that it depends on an intelligent, efficient cause.

Chance

Many natural phenomena are due to chance. Such, for example, are the shape of a particular mountain range, the location of pebbles on the seashore, or the number of individuals in a particular species. But not all natural phenomena are of this kind.

To perceive the difference, it suffices to consider what is meant by a chance effect.

A chance effect is *an effect which results from the conjunction of an uncoordinated plurality of causes.*

A typical chance effect is the appearance of the winning number in a lottery. Several lines of causation, each independent of the other—the numbering of the marbles, the rotation of the numbered marbles in the barrel and the insertion of an instrument to pick up one of them—meet at a point by chance. The various causes are *uncoordinated.*

When several causes are *coordinated,* the result is not due to chance. Such is the emergence of a chicken from an egg. There are various factors at work in the egg, and these, combined with the activity of the sitting hen, are coordinated so as to bring about the appearance of the chicken at the end of the period of incubation.

It is because the factors responsible for a chance effect are uncoordinated that chance effects are essentially variable. Where the causes are coordinated, the effects are invariable, being brought about by *natures* ordained to produce such effects. Chance, being the result of the absence of coordination in the causes, is essentially negative and therefore the chance effect is a superficial phenomenon in a universe that is governed by law.

The universe, in a word, is intelligible only as a universe of natures, each of which is ordained to produce the effects that are proper to it, and such ordering requires an intelligent cause to account for it.

Additional Remarks

1. Kant argued that even if the argument from order were valid, it would establish only the existence of a finite intelligence. To refute Kant's objection, it is necessary to consider the relation that exists between *intelligence* and

its object, which is *being*. The intelligence is in possession of truth when it knows that which is. The proportionate object of a finite intelligence will be finite being. If we are to account for such an ordering we must come ultimately to an intelligence that is identical with its own being; and such an intelligence is infinite.

2. In his book *Luck or Cunning?* published in 1867, Samuel Butler refuted Darwinism. Luck or cunning, Butler pointed out, are the only alternatives, and since the first is absurd, it must follow that the universe is the work of cunning, or intelligence.

Henri Bergson refuted Darwinism in his book *Creative Evolution,* and L. S. Berg, an eminent ichthyologist, did the same in his book *Nomogenesis, or Evolution Determined by Law.*

3. In his book *Chance and Necessity,* published in 1970, Jacques Monod, an eminent biologist, argued that natural selection operates on mutations that have been produced by chance, but that once the chance mutation is inserted in the structure of the DNA molecule, it is removed from the field of pure chance and enters that of necessity. But Monod faces the same difficulty as Empedocles, for he cannot explain why the DNA molecule is under the necessity of giving rise to an identical pattern in the offspring.

F. The Argument from Moral Order

This argument, sometimes called the *Argument from Conscience,* has pride of place in Cardinal Newman's religious thought. He attached less weight to arguments based on a consideration of the visible universe, because he was not acquainted with St. Thomas' Realist theory of knowledge, his own philosophy being an Empiricist Subjectivism derived from John Locke.

The starting point of the argument is the fact of experience that we are aware of moral obligations of which we are not the author. It can be formulated thus:

Every man who comes to the use of reason knows

that in his free acts he is subject to a moral law—he is under a moral obligation to do some things and avoid others. In a word, he is aware of a moral order which he apprehends, but does not create.

Such an order must have an intelligent cause, and as with the order in the visible universe, this cause must ultimately be the supreme intelligent cause, who is an end unto himself.

Comments.

1. This argument from the "voice of conscience" is valid, but since it starts from our conscious state, it is a subsidiary argument, and it depends for its effectiveness on the moral sensitivity of those to whom it is addressed.

2. In the *Summa Theologiae* (I-II, q.2), St. Thomas argues that if man is to be true to his nature as a moral agent, the supreme objective of his endeavor cannot be any created good, but only God, the Uncreated Good.

3. It is impossible to give an intelligible account of a natural right which belongs to man by reason of the fact that he is a human being and not as a concession from the State, if we do not base his possession of this right on his orientation to God, his Ultimate End.

Having a moral obligation to seek God as his Ultimate End, he has from God the right to the necessary means of seeking this end, such as the free use of his faculties and to his life, the indispensable conditions for this activity.

These rights must be respected by other human beings if they in their turn are to be rightly oriented to the same Ultimate End.

In any other explanation of right, such as the Positivist or the Utilitarian, the concept is emptied of its content.

The Problem of Evil

It is not easy to reconcile the existence of God with the presence of evil in the world. St. Thomas was well aware of the difficulty in the *Summa Theologiae* and set it down as the first objection to his thesis that God exists. He wrote: "If God exists, He must be infinite goodness. Now infinite goodness is incompatible with evil. But it is a fact that there is evil in the world. Therefore God does not exist." Epicurus and others have put the objection in the form of a dilemma: "If evil exists, it must be either because God is unable to prevent it or is unwilling to do so. If He is unable to prevent it, He is not omnipotent. If He is unwilling to do so, He is not infinitely good. In either case, the conclusion is that God, as traditional theism represents Him, does not exist."

To deal with the difficulty, we must consider what is meant by evil. Evil is not a positive entity, but is real. It is a real privation, that is, it is the absence of some perfection (i.e., some quality or property) in a being which ought to have it. It may be physical or moral.

Physical evil consists in the absence of some property in a body which ought to have it. Thus blindness in man is a physical evil, because nature intends that he should have his sight. To be unable to see is not an evil for an oyster, because it is not endowed by nature with the power of vision.

Moral evil is found only in beings endowed with freedom, and it consists in the absence of right order in some action that is performed freely. Thus an act of theft is morally evil, because it is the taking of an object that belongs to another. This is in contravention of the right order, which demands that property rights be respected.

Notes:

1. Evil is a problem only for the theist. It is not a problem for the atheist, for if God does not exist, there is no reason why there should not be physical and moral evil in the world.

2. No theist maintains that the problem of evil, and particularly moral evil, can be satisfactorily solved.

   We are confronted here with what St. Paul calls "the mystery of lawlessness" (2 Thes. 2:7). We cannot say why God permits moral evil. But clearly He does so, and since He is infinite goodness, we may be certain that He does so in order that the evil may serve as an occasion for the attainment of some greater good.

Thus our redemption was accomplished by Christ's patient acceptance of His sufferings and death at the hands of evil men. But often we cannot say what the greater good is, or how the evil contributes to its attainment, since we are in the dark regarding the details of God's providential plan.

To prevent physical evil, God would have to intervene constantly to prevent physical causes from producing their natural effects. Constant miraculous intervention of this kind is incompatible with the maintenance of the order of nature which requires that natural causes produce the effects to which they are ordained.

3. Concentration on the evil in the world may lead one to overlook the presence of finite good. Finite good, as we have seen, implies the ordering of means to ends, for something is said to be good for an agent either because it is the end to which it is ordained, or is a means contributing to its attainment of this end. And the ordering of means to ends requires an intelligent first efficient cause to account for it.

4. St. Thomas has pointed out that if we say evil exists, we must admit that God exists. For since evil is the privation of some good which a being ought to have, it is intelligible only if the being in question is ordained to the good which it lacks, such as vision in the case of an animal that is blind. If the relationship to good is removed, there will be an absence of some reality, but this absence will not be evil. Evil therefore implies the existence of order and order requires an intelligent efficient cause to account for it.

The Possibility of Revelation, Prophecy, and Miracles

Can God reveal truth to man by speaking to him and certify that this revelation has taken place by working miracles and seeing that prophecies are fulfilled? How we answer these questions will depend on our views regarding the relationship of the universe to God, its First Efficient Cause.

A. Revelation

Since God, the cause of order in the universe, is Supreme Intelligence, He must be able to devise means of revealing Himself to man over and above the visible creation, which bears witness to His wisdom and power, should He wish to do so. It would be absurd to suppose that He could not act directly on the human mind, communicating truths to it and so enlightening it that it received, together with the truths communicated, the certain knowledge that it was God who was communicating them.

Direct revelation of this kind was claimed by Moses and the prophets in the Old Testament and by Christ and His Apostles in the New; but it is not available to everyone.

Whether the revelation which is presented as coming from God really comes from Him can be determined to some extent by examining its content, but the decisive criteria are the prophecies and miracles which guarantee that it is authentic. But are prophecies and miracles possible?

B. Prophecy

It is evident that events which for us are future are known by God before they occur. If they were not, He would undergo change, passing from ignorance to knowledge, which is incompatible with His infinite perfection.

Existing in His eternity, God has present to His mind everything that takes place, whether it be past, present, or future, so that what is future for us is present to Him. The divine knowledge of future events, communicated to the prophet and expounded by him comes to the hearers as a prophecy of what is to come. When the prophecy has been fulfilled, it serves to guarantee the authenticity of the revelation to which it was attached.

C. Miracles

A *miracle* is an event, perceived by the senses, which, being quite beyond the power of natural causes is brought about by direct intervention of God and serves as a warranty for some religious truth.

As the First Efficient Cause of all created being, God is omnipotent, that is, He is able to confer existence on any reality that can be, i.e., any reality that would not involve a contradiction such as a square circle.

But the effect of a miraculous intervention on the part of God, such as the restoration of a dead body to life, does not involve a contradiction, and therefore such an intervention is possible. However, the possibility of a miracle will be clearer if we set out in more detail the Theistic conception of the relationship of the universe to God.

1. God created the universe out of nothing, that is, without making use of any pre-existing material. If there were any such pre-existing material, it would possess existence of itself, that is, it would be necessary being. And this is impossible, for all reality other than God is contingent.

2. Created out of nothing by God, the universe is essentially contingent and therefore depends on God for its continuance in existence.

3. Since the actions of created causes are a form of contingent being, they must depend on God for their coming into being and their continuance in being. Created causes are truly active in the production of their effects, but they act in dependence on God, the First Efficient Cause.

4. As the First Cause of order in the universe, God governs it in accordance with a providential plan, which takes account of the interaction of the created causes of which the universe is composed.

Since the universe and all the beings in it depend completely on the Creator, it is clear that He can, if He chooses, intervene directly to bring about some miraculous effect, either by preventing the created cause from producing its natural effect or by bringing about some effect that is beyond the power of created causes.

Thus He is able, by a miraculous intervention, to bring it about that fire does not burn or a dead body returns to life.

D. The Discernibility of Miracles

Granted that miracles are possible, can we be certain that a given phenomenon is so far beyond the power of created cause that it must be attributed to the direct intervention of God?

It is true that our knowledge of the forces of nature is imperfect, so that what in one age would be regarded as beyond the power of the forces of nature may be found later to be within their range, e.g., a voyage to the moon and back, or witnessing events as they occur thousands of miles away.

But in some cases we can be certain that the event in question is miraculous. The raising of a dead body to life is beyond the power of natural causes, and the same must be said of instantaneous cures of organic diseases. So the raising of Lazarus and some of the cures wrought at Lourdes must be reckoned as genuine miracles.

Since the apparitions in 1858, there have been thousands of cures at Lourdes. Already in 1858, Dr. Dozous had made a list of more than a hundred. Subsequently a Medical Bureau was established, which recorded the medical details of the patient's illness, the time and circumstances of the cure and the subsequent medical history of the patient.

Alexis Carrel, the eminent biologist, has recorded how in 1902, he witnessed the cure of Marie Bailly, a cure which he declared to be quite inexplicable by natural causes.

In 1954, Dr. Vallet, the Director of the Medical Bureau, established the International Medical Committee, which in 1973, had 15,000 members and associates. Its central committee has met on six occasions between 1954 and 1978, and passed judgment on cases submitted to it by the Medical Bureau. It has passed on twenty-eight cases to the ecclesiastical authorities as worthy of consideration, and nineteen of these have been recognized by these authorities as miraculous.

It has been objected that if miracles were possible, the scientist could not do his work, since he could not be sure that his investigations would not be nullified by a miracle.

This objection has little force, since miracles occur so rarely that the scientist can proceed with his experiments with the moral certitude that they will not be rendered ineffectual by a miracle. Moreover, the purpose of a miracle is to promote some spiritual good and the frustration of a scientific experiment would not have this effect.

To discern whether a particular event is miraculous, that it is due to the direct intervention of God, we have to take account not only of the fact, but also its circumstances. As Cardinal Prospero Lambertini (later Pope Benedict XIV) pointed out in his treatise on beatification and canonization, we have first to make sure that the cure has no natural explanation and then ask whether the circumstances are such that it will serve to promote the glory of God and not merely foster idle curiosity.

The evil spirits are capable of producing effects that are beyond the power of man, e.g., they can withdraw the body of a medium from subjection to the law of gravity, as they seem to have done for the famous medium, D. D. Home, in 1868. But a consideration of all the circumstances will reveal that such phenomena are not the work of God and therefore not to be accounted as truly miraculous.

Note

1. *The God of Reason,* Burnes and Oates, London, 1961.

References

St. Thomas Aquinas, *Summa Theologiae,* I. qq.1-13; *Summa contra Gentiles,* I. chs. 10-13

R. Garrigou-Lagrange, O.P., *God, His Existence and Nature* (tr. B. Rose), Herder, St. Louis, 1935.
This is the most thorough treatment by a modern scholar of the philosophical theology of St. Thomas. It does not figure in Hans Küng's bibliography.

R. P. Phillips, *Modern Thomistic Philosophy,* Burns and Oates, London, 1935. Vol. II, chs. 1-3, contain a succinct account of the Thomistic proofs of the existence of God.

E. L. Mascall, *He Who Is: A Study in Traditional Theism,* Darton, Longman and Todd, London, 1943. A full and critical account of the "five ways" by an Anglican scholar.

E. Gilson, *God and Philosophy,* Yale University Press, New Haven, 1941. In four lectures, Gilson, a leading historian of philosophy, shows how the problem of God has been variously tackled in Greek, Christian, Modern and Contemporary philosophy, and indicates how the key to a solution is to be found by taking seriously the actuality of the act of existence.

James Collins, *God in Modern Philosophy,* Henry Regnery, Chicago, 1959. Probably the most thorough account in English of the development of philosophical theology from Nicholas Cusanus (d. 1464) to the present day.

Hans Küng, *Does God Exist?* Collins, London, 1980. Küng confines his discussion of the question to modern philosophy, beginning with Descartes, and he ends with the fideist conclusion that the existence of God cannot be proven by reason but must be accepted as the only alternative to nihilism.

Germain Grisez, *Beyond the New Theism: A Philosophy of Religion,* University of Notre Dame, Indiana, 1975. Grisez develops the argument from contingency, and refutes the various modern philosophical systems that rule out the possibility of a natural theology.

Readings in Natural Theology, selected by Jules A. Baisnee, S. S., Newman, Westminster, MD, 1965. This is a useful collection of quotations from authors, ancient and modern, on the existence and nature of God.

Anthony Kenny, *The Five Ways: St. Thomas Aquinas' Proofs of God's Existence,* Routtedge and Regan Paul, London, 1969. Kenny, who holds that the predicate "is" is at best uninformative and at worst unintelligible, has no understanding of what Thomistic metaphysics is all about.

R. Jastrow, *God and the Astronomers,* W. W. Norton, New York, 1978. Jastrow sets out the evidence which seems to indicate that our universe came into existence between 10 and 20 billion years ago.

C. Tresmontant, *Comment Se Pose Aujourd'hui le Probleme de L'existence de Dieu?* Le Seuil, Paris, 1966. Tresmontant shows how the Realism of Aristotle is able to cope with the facts discovered by modern astronomy and biology.

A. Olivieri and B. Bernard Billet, *Y A-t-il Encore des Miracles à Lourdes?* Lethielleux, Paris, 1979.
The authors, a doctor of medicine and a theologian, discuss the dossiers of twenty-one cures, which occurred between 1949 and 1978.

St. Thomas Aquinas, *Summa Theologiae* I, q.85, a.2, contains a classical statement of the position of Natural Realism, viz., that the concept formed by the intellect is not *that which* is known but *that by which* the intellect knows the extra-mental object.

IV. The New Testament as a Source of Genuine Historical Information about Christ

"Can a man, as a civilized being, as a European, believe at all, that is, believe in the divinity of the Son of God, Jesus Christ, for therein, strictly speaking, rests the whole faith?" This is the question which the hero puts to himself in Doestoevsky's draft of his novel *The Possessed.*

How one answers this question will depend in great measure on the value one attaches to the New Testament documents as sources of historical information about Christ, for there can be little doubt that "the faith of the Church stands or falls with the general reliability of the historical evidence for the life and death of Jesus Christ."[1]

There have been a few writers in this century (Drews, Couchoud, Wells) who have held that Christ is a wholly mythical figure who never existed at all. He would have been the product of the creative imagination of some early Christian writers seeking to embody in a human person the myth of man's reconciliation with the Deity. This theory is so evidently false that few scholars bother to refute it, but it is of historical interest because Lenin read Drews' book and adopted his theory. As a consequence, it was for a long time the party line in Soviet Russia that Christ was a mythical figure and not a historical personage. This view of the matter has in recent years been set aside in some

Russian scholarly journals, but it is still to be found in various official Soviet publications.

The Views of Renan, Bultmann, and Second Vatican Council

Ernest Renan (d. 1892) and Adolf Harnack (d. 1930) held that the New Testament contains a great deal of genuine historical information about Christ, but alongside this genuine material, there are supernatural elements, such as accounts of miraculous happenings, which cannot be accepted as historical. As it turned out, this naturalistic interpretation of the Gospel story broke down and had to be abandoned, for if the supernatural element is eliminated, the whole story becomes unintelligible. Why, one writer asked, would the Jewish authorities have been so anxious to do away with Christ, if, as Renan and Harnack held, He was no more that a sentimental evangelist preaching the Fatherhood of God and the brotherhood of men?

Rudolf Bultmann (d. 1976), probably the most influential New Testament scholar of the twentieth century, maintained that Christ is a vague, shadowy figure like Buddha or Pythagoras, so enveloped in legend that His true lineaments are indiscernible. The only certain information that can be gotten from the New Testament records is that a man called Jesus of Nazareth existed and was crucified on the orders of Pontius Pilate. "I do indeed think," Bultmann wrote, "that we can know almost nothing of the life and personality of Jesus, since the early Christian sources show no interest in either, are moreover fragmentary and often legendary; and other sources of information about Jesus do not exist." [2] For Bultmann, this lack of historical information about Christ does not matter, since it is enough that Christ be a model of existential authenticity for the Christian believer in the twentieth century.

André Feuillet has pointed out that Bultmann's scepticism regarding the New Testament documents has its roots in his philosophical and theological views. It is not a conclusion based on literary and historical criticism, but is a corollary to his Lutheran distrust of the role of the intellect in religious matters, his acceptance of modern thought as the norm of what elements of the Gospel message we can accept and his adoption of Heidegger's Existentialism as the key to the understanding of reality.[3]

Some of Bultmann's disciples, e.g., Ernest Käsemann and Gunther Bornkamm, hold that we can get much more information about Christ from the New Testament than Bultmann would allow, but they are still profoundly affected by Bultmann's scepticism. Bornkamm, for example, rejects John's testimony to an early ministry in Judea, maintains that Christ did not refer to Himself as the Son of Man, and considers that the Gospel accounts of the trial and death of Jesus are of little historical value. Wolfhart Pannenberg, another post-Bultmannian, rejects as not authentic the three predictions of the Passion, and treats the accounts of the raising of the widow's son at Naim and of Lazarus as "more or less late and legendary stories."

The Importance of Historical Fact for Christianity

The orthodox Christian view is that the Gospels provide us with a great deal of genuine historical information about the life and teachings of Christ, culminating in the account of His passion, death and resurrection. "Holy Mother Church," the Second Vatican Council declared, "has firmly and with absolute constancy maintained and continues to maintain that the four Gospels, whose historicity she unhesitatingly affirms, hand on what Jesus, the Son of God, while He lived among men, really did and taught, for their eternal salvation, until the day He was taken up."[4]

This does not mean that the Gospel record is history as the modern historian writes it. For one thing, it does not provide us with precise details of time and place, and the order of events is only roughly chronological. In the second place, it is not a purely objective, disinterested account of what Christ said and did, but was compiled by believers to bring men to faith in Christ or to confirm believers in their faith. What the evangelists provide is a record of the acts of God in history as He wrought our salvation; but this salvation depends, not on "cleverly devised myths" (2 Pt. 1:16), but on events that really happened. This is what the Church means when she unhesitatingly proclaims the historicity of the four Gospels.

This insistence on the importance of historical fact is one of the features that distinguish Christianity from such religions as Buddhism and Islam. The teaching of Buddha and Mohammed is independent of their life and would not be notably different if it were proven that they had never existed. For the Muslims, Mohammed was but the privileged instrument of God, used by Him to reveal the Koran, which was pre-existent from eternity in heaven and revealed bit by bit to Mohammed. Hence if he vanished in myth, the equilibrium of Islam would not theoretically be greatly affected. With Christianity it is different, for Christ Himself is the center of the Christian religion. The Christian Faith is faith in Christ, Christian worship is the worship of Christ, and Christian moral life is the imitation of Christ. Hence St. Paul could sum up his preaching in the phrase, "We preach Christ crucified" (1 Cor. 1:23).

Some have said that all that is needed as a basis for our Christian Faith is our present experience of the risen Christ. The four evangelists did not share this view, for they were at pains to provide us with information regarding His public ministry. He who was crucified and rose from the dead was none other than the Jesus of Nazareth who for three years went about Galilee and Judea, preaching, healing the sick, driving out evil spirits and gathering around Him a group of disciples, to some of whom He gave the task of spreading the good news of the kingdom of God. St. Luke, for example, in the opening verses of his Gospel makes it clear that he intends to provide Theophilus with genuine historical information about Christ, in order that he may have certain knowledge of the facts on which his faith is based. St. Luke, therefore, did not regard it as derogatory to faith to make it depend on historical fact. Bultmann and others have held that to tie faith thus closely to the facts of history is to make faith precarious, since historical knowledge is subject to constant revision. But some historical facts are so well established as to be beyond the possibility of doubt, and hence the essential connection of the historical facts regarding Jesus with the Christian Faith does not make that Faith precarious. So we find that St. Peter in his address to the Jews at Pentecost (Acts 2:32-38) did not hesitate to put forward the fact of the Resurrection as his warrant for calling on his hearers to believe in Christ.

The Authenticity
of the New Testament Documents

The New Testament documents as we now have them are attributed by Christian tradition, since the second century, to various first-century writers, who were either Apostles or associates of the Apostles. But is this tradition to be accepted? Are these documents authentic? There are two questions here. First, does the text of the books which we now possess correspond with that of the originals, or has the text been greatly altered in the course of time? Second, were the original documents written by those to whom they are attributed?

In the nineteenth century, the Tübingen School of F. C. Baur (d. 1860) and his followers maintained that most of the New Testament documents were the work of second-century writers but were attributed to Apostles and Evangelists to give them more authority. They accepted as genuine only four of St. Paul's Epistles (Galatians, Romans, and 1 and 2 Corinthians), dismissing the rest as spurious, and relegating the remaining New Testament books to the second century, dating some as late as 150 A.D. This theory is now a museum piece, for it is generally agreed that all the books, with the possible exception of 2 Peter, date from the first century. Moreover, there is wide agreement that many of the books were written by the authors to whom they were attributed by tradition, although there are several about which there is no agreement.

How Close Is Our Present Text to the Original Autographs?

The original texts, which were on papyrus, have long since disappeared, but the New Testament scholar is much better placed than the scholar who is dealing with, for example, the Latin classics, for the texts at his disposal are much older and far more numerous than those available to the classical scholar. Thus the earliest text of *Caesar's Gallic War* is a MS of the ninth century, and the extant parts of the works of Tacitus are represented by two MSS, one of the ninth century and the other of the tenth.

It is a very different story for the MSS of the New Testament. These are counted in their thousands, and two of them, the *Codex Vaticanus* and the *Codex Sinaiticus,* date from the fourth century. Besides these complete codices, there are papyrus fragments from the second and third centuries. The earliest of these is a fragment containing some verses from the Gospel of St. John (18:31...38), which was found in Egypt and is dated around the year 130 by the experts.

Besides these New Testament texts, there are passages in the writings of the Apostolic Fathers which reveal an acquaintance with either the New Testament texts as we have them, or the oral tradition which these texts have preserved for us. Thus in the letters of St. Ignatius of Antioch, who was martyred about 110, there are passages which echo passages in the Gospels of St. Matthew and St. John and the Epistles of St. Paul. In the Epistle of Clement to the Church of Corinth, usually dated about 96, there are quotations from the Synoptic Gospels, the Epistles of St. Paul, and the Epistle to the Hebrews.

To these we can add the witness of the Gnostic heretics, who flourished in the middle of the second century and quoted the New Testament writings in support of their doctrines.

With these resources at their disposal, modern scholars are now able to establish a text which can be accepted as very close to what the original authors wrote. There are of course variant readings, but these bear mostly on matters of detail, and do not give rise to doubts about the New Testament witness to any important element of Christian faith or practice.

After a lifetime devoted to the study of the history of the New Testament text, Sir Frederic Kenyon wrote: "The interval between the dates of the original composition and the earliest extant evidence becomes so small as to be in fact negligible, and the last foundation for any doubt that the Scriptures have come down to us substantially as they were written has been removed. Both the authenticity and the general integrity of the books of the New Testament may be regarded as finally established."[5]

St. Paul

Of the twenty-seven books that make up the New Testament, the Epistles of St. Paul, if not the earliest, are among the earliest, the first being written about 50 and the last in the early 60's.

It has been said that St. Paul showed no interest in the earthly life of Christ, his whole attention being concentrated on the Risen Lord. This is a misinterpretation of the Apostle's words: "Even though we once regarded Christ from a human point of view, we regard him thus no longer" (2 Cor. 5:16). It is true that we do not find in his Epistles the detailed information which the Gospels provide, but it must be remembered that the Epistles mostly deal with issues that had arisen in the local Church, and they are addressed to Christians who already knew the Gospel story, at least in outline, since they had already been evangelized. Nevertheless, it is possible to draw from the Epistles an outline of the life of Christ and a portrait of the Master which tallies with the evidence provided by the Evangelists.

The Apostle does indeed assert the divine pre-existence of Christ (Phil. 2:5-11; Col. 1:15-17), but he also speaks of Him as a real human being. He is, the Apostle tells us, a descendant of Abraham and David, He lived under the Jewish law, was betrayed, and on the night of His betrayal instituted in bread and wine a memorial of His death, was crucified and rose again, and after His resurrection was seen by many witnesses. We find the Apostle quoting the Master's teaching on marriage and divorce, and on the right of preachers to have their material needs supplied. His moral teaching echoes that of the Sermon on the Mount, and he bases his appeal for Christian behavior on the example of Christ, who was meek and humble of heart and did not please Himself but sought always to please the Father.

From a careful reading of the Epistles, therefore, we can glean many items of historical information about Christ; but the fact remains that our main source of information is the four Gospels.

The Gospels

It was some decades after the Resurrection before the Gospel texts we now have were written, and during this time the story of the words and deeds of Jesus was handed on by word of mouth.

This does not mean that the story must have been distorted in the telling, for in those days when books were scarce and many people illiterate, great stress was laid on memorization. In a lecture given in Oxford in 1957, Harald Riesenfeld, a Swedish scholar, argued that it may be taken as certain that Jesus and His Apostles made use of the pedagogical methods that were in use in Palestine at the time. The content of Jesus' teaching was radically different from that of the Scribes and Pharisees, but there is good evidence that this teaching was set out quite early in systematic form, suitable for memorizing, and there are indications, too, that Jesus expected His disciples to memorize His teaching in the form in which He had given it.

Riesenfeld's argument was developed by Birger Gerhardsson in his book *Memory and Manuscript,* published in 1961. In this work he describes how the rabbis were expected to know the sacred text by heart and insisted that their pupils memorize their teaching, which was a commentary on the sacred text, so as to be able to repeat it verbatim. Gerhardsson's evidence, it is true, is drawn from the practice of the rabbinical schools in the early centuries of the Christian era, but it is a fair inference that the practice was not notably different in the time of Christ.

Gerhardsson then goes on to argue that if this is how Palestinian Jews were educated in the time of Christ we may take it as certain that Christ taught in this way. He writes: "Turning to Jesus' oral teaching, we must reckon with the fact that He used a method similar to that of Jewish—and Hellenistic—teachers: the scheme of text and interpretation. He must have made His disciples learn certain sayings by heart—if He taught, He must have required His disciples to memorize. This statement is not intended to be dogmatic or apologetic, but is a consideration based on a comparison with the comtemporary situation."[6]

Riesenfeld and Gerhardsson's thesis has been contested by scholars of the Bultmannian persuasion, but their objections have been effectively dealt with by the Swedish scholars, and in the opinion of Louis Bouyer, we may consider the case to be closed.[7]

It is certain that the Apostles had drawn up a brief systematic account easy to memorize, of the main events of the life of Christ from His baptism by John to the Resurrection. We find St. Peter setting out just such a summary account of these events in his speech when Cornelius was converted (Acts 10:37-43). This was the "Gospel tradition," a formula or set of formulas containing the essential elements of the Christian Faith. To this tradition St. Paul refers when he is writing to the Corinthians on the Eucharist and the Resurrection (1 Cor. 11:23; 15:3). It is interesting, Bouyer remarks, that "St. Paul introduces his narrative with terms that are the same technical words by which contemporary Jews qualified the transmission and faithful reception of a tradition emanating from an authoritative rabbi through a continuous chain of disciples."[8]

Since many of the early converts to the Christian Faith were literate, it can be taken as certain that parts of the Gospel story were put in writing quite early, and St. Luke begins his "ordered account" by telling us that when he wrote, many such documents were in existence.

The earliest witness to the authorship of the Gospels is Papias, bishop of Hierapolis, a city of Thrygia. Writing about 120, he tells us that the first Gospel to be written was that of Matthew, who wrote in the "Hebrew" (i.e., the Aramaic) tongue and the second was that of Mark, the "interpreter" of Peter. Of the Aramaic text of Matthew no trace remains; the Gospel of Matthew that we possess was written in Greek, and there are probable indications of its dependence on Mark.

The third Gospel was written by St. Luke, a convert from paganism, and the companion of St. Paul in the later stages of his ministry. Luke also wrote the Acts of the Apostles, a companion volume to the Gospel, which traces the expansion of Christianity from its beginnings in Jerusalem in 30, to St. Paul's imprisonment in Rome from 60-62. Luke almost certainly makes use of material from the Gospel of Mark, and he could well have become acquainted with it when he and Mark were together in Rome in the early 60's (cf. Col. 4:10, 14; Philem. 1:24).

That Mark and Luke wrote the Gospels which have been traditionally assigned to them is a fact which cannot be seriously questioned; what is less certain is when these Gospels were written.

The authorship and date of the Gospel of John we shall discuss in a later section.

The Date of Acts and the Synoptic Gospels

The question of the dating of the Gospels is not without its importance, for the closer they are in time to the facts they narrate, the greater the likelihood of their being an accurate account. "Dates," John A. T. Robinson writes, "remain disturbingly fundamental data."[9]

There is general agreement among scholars that Mark was written about 60, and a majority hold that Matthew and Luke were written in the 80's, Acts being written some time after the Gospel of Luke.

Since the Gospel of Luke and Acts may be regarded as two parts of a single work, Acts being a sequel to Luke, the dating of the two books constitutes a single question, the dating of Luke-Acts.

In his book *The Date of the Acts and of the Synoptic Gospels,* Harnack, probably the greatest historian of the New Testament period in modern times, explains how, after adopting the late dating of Acts, he became convinced that it was written in the early 60's, before the result of St. Paul's trial was known. He wrote: "The more clearly we see that the trial of St. Paul and above all his appeal to Caesar is the chief subject of the last quarter of the Acts, the more hopeless does it appear that we can explain why the narrative breaks off as it does, except by assuming that the trial has not yet actually reached its close."[10] This is corroborated by the absolute silence of Acts concerning everything that happened between 64 and 70 A.D., so he concludes that "it is in the highest degree probable that the work was written when St. Paul's trial in Rome had not yet come to an end."[11]

If this dating of Acts is right, the date of the Lukan Gospel must be earlier, and that of the Gospel of St. Mark earlier still. To assign Mark's Gospel to the late 50's is quite compatible with the evidence. St. Matthew's Gospel, in Harnack's opinion, must be placed in close proximity to the destruction of Jerusalem in 70, being assigned in its present shape to years immediately succeeding that catastrophe. (In Matthew 22:7 there is a reference to the burning of the city, an item which is not found in the parallel passage in Luke 14:16-24.)

John A. T. Robinson has accepted Harnack's case regarding the date of Luke and Acts, setting out the arguments and dealing with the objections that can be raised

against it.[12] The main objection to the earlier dating of
Luke is based on the fact that Luke's account of Christ as
He wept over Jerusalem seems to be colored by the events
of the siege of 70: "The days shall come upon you, when
your enemies will cast up a bank about you and surround
you, and hem you in on every side" (19:43). However, as
William Barclay has pointed out, this description of the
siege of Jerusalem corresponds exactly with what Pom-
pey's army had done in 63 B.C., an event with which every
Jew at the time of Christ was familiar.[13] So any prediction
of the capture of Jerusalem by the Romans would have
been couched in these terms.

As regards the dating of Matthew, Robinson gives several reasons for putting the date before 70, and he points
out that the reference to "fire" in 22:7 need not have been
inserted in the text after 70. He accepts the view of Reicke
that the situation presupposed by Matthew corresponds
with what is known about Christianity in Palestine between 50 and 64 A.D., and he suggests a date before 62,
when Symeon succeeded his brother James as bishop of
Jerusalem, James having been murdered by some Jews.
Symeon's name is not mentioned in the Gospel, and had
the Gospel been written after 62, it would probably have
appeared there. As an argument from silence, this has no
importance, but it is of some value as corroborating the
others.[14] Robinson holds that the Gospels in the form in
which we have them are the end result of what we might
anachronistically call several editions, Luke being an
exception, since it is the nearest equivalent to a modern
book written and published for a single individual and at a
particular moment in time. He concludes that the text of
Mark that has reached us dates from the late 50's, while
Matthew and Luke date from the early 60's.[15]

When one has read Robinson's closely reasoned case,
one must agree with C. H. Dodd when he writes that
much of the late dating of the New Testament documents
is quite arbitrary, even wanton, the offspring not of any
argument that can be presented but rather of the prejudice

that anyone who assents to the traditional position of the early Church will be dismissed as a stick-in-the-mud.[16]

The Gospel of St. John

The Identity of the Author

Is John the Apostle and the son of Zebedee the author of this Gospel which bears his name? As M. J. Lagrange, the great biblical scholar remarks, this is an important question, because if it is answered in the affirmative, the value of the Gospel as a historical document is greatly enhanced, for this would make it the testimony of an eye-witness who was closely involved in the events he narrates.

It was universally admitted until the end of the 18th century that John the Apostle was the author, but now there are many scholars, Catholic as well as non-Catholic, who question this attribution. However, the case for the affirmative is very strong. It was ably stated by Wescott, in his classical commentary on the Gospel, published in 1885, by Sanday, Drummond, Stanton at the turn of the century, and accepted as the most probable view by such recent writers as Stauffer, Headlam, Barclay, and John A. T. Robinson. The argument is two-fold—the witness of tradition, and the text of the Gospel itself.

A. The Witness of Tradition

This was well summed up by Sanday, "In regard to the external evidence," he writes, "I would not spend my time in refinements upon some of the scanty details furnished by the scanty literature of the first half of the second century. I would rather take my stand on the state of things revealed to us on the lifting of the curtain for that scene of the Church's history which extends roughly from about the year 170 to 200. I would invite attention to the distribution of the evidence in this period: Irenaeus and the Letter of the Churches of Vienna and Lyons in Gaul, Heracleon in Italy, Tertullian at Carthage, Polycrates at Ephesus, Theophilus at Antioch, Tatian at Rome and in Syria, Clement at Alexandria. The strategical positions are occupied, one might say, all over the Empire. In the great majority of cases there is not a hint of dissent. On the contrary, the fourfold Gospel is regarded for the most part as one and indivisible." [17] St. Irenaeus (c. 180) is a particularly authoritative witness because he was a disciple of St. Polycarp, who himself was a disciple of St. John. The testimony of Irenaeus has been challenged, but the attempts to weaken it rest on several misconceptions. "Critics speak of Irenaeus," Drummond wrote, "as though he had fallen out of the moon, paid two or three visits to Polycarp's lecture-room and never known anyone else. In fact, he must have known all sorts of men, of all ages, both in the East and the West, and among others his venerable predecessor Pothinus, who was upward of ninety at the time of his death. He must have had numerous links with the early part of the century." [18]

Barclay thus sets out what can be gathered from the documents of tradition: "To sum up, the fourth Gospel was written by John, who was the beloved disciple and an Apostle; it was written at Ephesus; it was the last of the Gospels to be written; and there are indications that the Christian community had a vital share in the projecting of it and perhaps even in the writing of it. Such is the account that tradition gives us of the fourth Gospel." [19]

B. The Internal Evidence

The classical statement of the case for genuineness based on internal evidence was stated by B. F. Wescott in five ever-narrowing propositions:

1. The Fourth Gospel Was Written by a Jew

This is clear from his familiarity with the thought of the Old Testament, with Jewish customs, and the Jewish outlook on a host of items. If he speaks of "the Jews" who rejected Christ as if he were not one of them, this is accounted for by the fact that when he wrote there was already a gulf between the Church and the Synagogue. Indeed, St. Paul speaks in the same way about "the Jews" in 1 Thessalonians (2:14), written about 50.

2. The Writer Was a Jew of Palestine

His local knowledge of the geography of Palestine and the topography of Jerusalem is detailed and accurate, such as only a local inhabitant would possess. What is impressive is not only that he gets the facts right, but the way in which he incorporates them in his narrative. Drummond makes the point *apropos* the scene by the well in Samaria: "The writer knows the situation of Jacob's well, and that it is deep. He knows that there was a mountain close by, where the Samaritans worshiped. He knows that there were cornfields in the neighborhood. Every feature is true to the locality; yet nothing is described. It is the woman who lets us know the depth of the well and the presence of the mountain; and it is Jesus who alludes to the cornfields to illustrate his discourse. We are not told the name of the mountain or that the Samaritans had a temple there. There is a total absence of the art of a distant narrator. The author seems to have vividly before his own mind the scene which he knew so well in former days and is quick to forget that his readers cannot possibly know it as well as he does himself. This mode of treatment appears to me to be a strong evidence of first-hand knowledge."[20]

3. The Author Was an Eyewitness of the Events He Describes

In several places he explicitly claims to have first-hand knowledge of the facts (19:35; 21:24, cf. 1:14; 1 Jn. 1:1-3). As Sanday points out, this is a different matter from ordinary pseudonymous writing. These direct and strong assertions are either true or they are deliberate falsehoods, and there is little doubt about which of the alternatives we must choose.

Moreover, there is in the fourth Gospel a wealth of detail which can hardly be explained as anything other than the personal recollections of an eyewitness. Besides the incident in Samaria to which we have referred, there is a regular mention of the great Jewish feasts, as these mark the progression of the public ministry of Christ, e.g., the

Feast of Tabernacles (10:22), when, because it was winter, He took shelter in Solomon's portico. There are detailed notices of time, not only of the day, but also of the hour, not because the story depends on these, but because so it was. There is a gallery of characters who come alive in this Gospel and who without this material would be little more than names: Andrew, Philip, Nathanael, Martha and Mary. We are told that the loaves on which the multitudes were fed were *barley* loaves (6:9); the house was filled with the fragrance of the ointment (12:3); the clothes in the grave were lying as if the body had evaporated out of them (20:6-7).

4. The Writer Was an Apostle

He is in possession of facts that would be known only to an Apostle, such as their thoughts at critical times in the ministry of Jesus, and the subject of their conversation when no one else was there.

5. The Writer Was John, the Son of Zebedee, Who Was Also the Beloved Disciple

The writer claims to be specially intimate with the mind and heart of Jesus. Now it is clear from the Synoptic Gospels that three of the Apostles (Peter, James and John) formed an inner circle of the apostolic group. James was put to death by Herod Agrippa I in 42, and Peter by Nero in 65, before the fourth Gospel was written.

The Apostle John is never mentioned by name in the Gospel, and the author is meticulous about names. The only John he mentions is John the Baptist, who is referred to simply as "John." If he refers to himself as "the disciple whom Jesus loved," this need not bespeak pride. The closeness of his relationship with Jesus guarantees the reliability of his testimony, and if he mentions the relationship, it is surely with wondering gratitude.

Those who contend that John was not the author have put forward a number of other candidates, including John

Mark, and Lazarus, but none of these is really likely. One such is John the Elder, who may have been referred to by Papias as a personage distinct from the Apostle. But, as John A. T. Robinson remarks, "It does not help to bring in the shadowy figure of John the Elder, who, even if he were separate from the Apostle, is nowhere stated to have been a disciple of John the son of Zebedee, or *(pace* Eusebius) to have lived in Ephesus, or indeed to have written a word, though Eusebius *guessed* that he could have written the Apocalypse." [21]

William Barclay, who devotes 107 pages to the problem, comes to the following conclusion: "So, after traveling the long way round, it seems to me that in the end there is no better candidate for the authorship of the fourth Gospel than John the Apostle. That he could not have written it on the grounds of intellectual ability or personal quality is a statement no one can make as a certainty. That he called himself the disciple whom Jesus loved could be the outcome of astonished humility rather than of pride. That Irenaeus was mistaken is not and cannot be proven, and that he led everyone else away on the same mistaken track as himself is next door to incredible. Above all there is the unbroken and almost unwavering tradition, which cannot be lightly disregarded, unless a better candidate for authorship is produced." [22]

André Feuillet, a leading Catholic biblical scholar, is of the opinion that the Catholic Church is committed to maintaining the apostolic origin of the fourth Gospel. He writes: "Catholic exegesis tends more and more to abandon the apostolic origin and historicity of the Gospel of John: it would not be an apostolic witness nor a source of historical information about Jesus, but only a theological document—of the first importance, it is true. For my part, I do not think that the Catholic Church can ever come to read the Gospel in this way." [23]

C. The Date of the Gospel

The Tubingen School of F. C. Baur put the writing of the fourth Gospel in the middle of the second century. This dating has now been abandoned by everyone and it is the general view that it was written toward the end of the first century, some years before the death of the Apostle, which according to an early tradition occurred in the reign of Trajan (98-117).

John A. T. Robinson has argued that it was written before 70, and he points out that external testimony to a later date is meager. He adds that there is nothing in the Gospel to indicate that Jerusalem has been destroyed and the Temple in ruins, and the reference to excommunication in 9:22 will fit well enough into the situation as it was before 70. The theology of the Gospel is indeed profound, but this need not presuppose a long period of development, for we find an advanced theology in the Epistles of St. Paul, which date from the 50's and early 60's.[24]

Whether the Gospel was written before 70, as Robinson holds, or toward the end of the century, the interval between the events it narrates and the composition of the document is too short for the transformation of Jesus into a mythical figure like Isis or Mithra.

D. The Historical Value of the Fourth Gospel

In the early decades of this century, the Gospel of St. John was dismissed as the meditations of a mystic having little basis in historical fact. So Kirsopp Lake wrote, "John may contain a few fragments of true tradition, but in the main it is fiction." This view has now been completely abandoned. In 1963, C. H. Dodd put forward what he maintained was a formidable case for the conclusion that "behind the fourth Gospel lies an ancient tradition independent of the other Gospels, and meriting serious consideration as a contribution to our knowledge of the historical facts concerning Jesus Christ."[25] Not only does the fourth Gospel supplement the information provided by the Synoptic Gospels, it is, in the opinion of John A. T. Robinson, "our single most reliable guide to the

exceedingly intricate (and historically unrepeatable) relationships between the 'spiritual' and the 'political' in the
ministry, trial and death of Jesus." [26]

St. John adds a great deal of information to the stream-
lined account of the ministry of Jesus which the Synoptics
provide. Thus, he has a much fuller account of the ministry of John the Baptist, speaks of an early ministry of Jesus
in southern Palestine and of a ministry of some months in
Jerusalem and Perea before the final week in Jerusalem.

This information provided by St. John, combined
with hints to be found in the Gospel of St. Mark, enable us
to give a much more intelligible account of the ministry of
Jesus than could be derived from the Synoptic Gospels
alone. A. M. Hunter has shown how the material from
these disparate sources can be woven into a coherent
whole. [27]

As regards the sayings of Jesus in the Gospel of
St. John, A. M. Hunter has set out the argument for their
substantial authenticity, and comments that it shows how
far modern scholarship has departed from the judgment of
Renan: "If Jesus spoke as Matthew represents, he cannot
have spoken as John relates." The debates with the Jewish
leaders in Jerusalem recorded by St. John do indeed differ
widely from the discourses to the simple folk in Galilee,
but this may be accounted for in part by the difference in
the audiences; and Israel Abrahams, a noted rabbinical
scholar, has pointed out that the Gospel accounts of the
debates with the Jewish leaders fit in well with the style of
argumentation prevalent in Jewish circles at the time. No
one maintains that what we have is a stenographic record,
but we may take it as a fair account of what Christ and His
adversaries said. [28]

In the introduction to the series of radio plays entitled
The Man Born To Be King, Dorothy Sayers bears witness
to the impact that St. John's Gospel had on her as she
grappled with the problem of creating a radio play from
the Gospel texts. "It must be remembered," she wrote,
"that of the four Evangels, St. John's is the only one that
claims to be the direct report of an eyewitness. And to

anyone accustomed to the imaginative handling of documents, the internal evidence bears out this claim. The Synoptists, on the whole, report the 'set pieces'; it is St. John who reports the words and actions of the individual, unrepeated occasion, retrieving them from the storehouse of trained memory which among people not made forgetful by pen and ink, replaces the filed records and the stenographer's notebook." [29]

Reasons for Accepting the Gospels as Historically Reliable

As a form of literature, the Gospels are unique, for they were written by believers to confirm the readers in their faith or to bring to faith those who did not yet believe. But because the Christian Faith is rooted in history, the evangelists were concerned to report what actually happened, and therefore the religious aim of the Gospels is not a valid reason for rejecting them as historically unreliable. "The presence of an interpretative element in the Gospel records," Anderson writes, "does not necessarily preclude their historical reliability or distort the picture which they give of the central figure." [30]

1. Two evangelists explicitly claim that they are reporting historical facts. St. Luke begins his Gospel by telling us that he has been at pains to gather reliable information about the events he intends to chronicle in order that Theophilus, for whom he is directly writing, may rest assured that his faith in Christ is based on well-established fact. The order in which he recounts the facts is not strictly chronological, but in its main outlines Luke's account of the public ministry of Jesus tallies with those of Matthew and Mark. St. John also presents his Gospel as a record of facts which serve as a warranty for faith in Christ (cf. 20:31).

2. The evangelists, even had they wanted to, could not have made up the story, for the central.figure is so tremendous and the story of His life so strange as to be beyond the power of human invention. John Stuart Mill, a

Rationalist thinker who rejected the supernatural, made this point when he wrote that it is useless "to say that Christ, as exhibited in the Gospels, is not historical and that we know not how much of what is admirable has been superadded by the tradition of His followers. Who among His disciples or among their proselytes was capable of inventing the sayings of Jesus or of imagining the life and character revealed in the Gospels? Certainly not the fishermen of Galilee; as certainly not St. Paul, whose character and idiosyncrasies were of a totally different sort; still less the early Christian writers."[31]

The Jews were expecting a Messiah, but not a suffering Messiah, and still less an Incarnate Deity. And even if they had guessed that the Messiah was to be the Son of God, it would never have crossed their minds that He would be born in a stable, spend thirty years in obscurity as a carpenter in an out-of-the-way village, and end His days on a cross outside Jerusalem. A crucified Messiah was so far outside the range of Jewish expectations, that He was for them in St. Paul's words (1 Cor. 1:23) a "stumbling block" on the path to faith.

3. The Gospels had to pass the scrutiny of men who had witnessed the events they recorded, and were hostile to the Christian claims.

The oral tradition incorporated in the Gospels was formulated when many who knew the facts were still alive and could have challenged statements that were demonstrably false. And if, as we have argued, the Synoptic Gospels were written before 70, many of these witnesses were still alive when these documents were written. "Scrupulous regard for fact," Léon-Dufour has written, "was almost a passion in the early Church."[32] It had to be so, because the early Christians were bearing witness to the truth, and their witness would have been worthless had they been shown to be impostors.

4. Historical and archaeological research have revealed that the Gospels depict with striking exactitude the very complex social and political order that prevailed in Palestine in the third decade of the first century, an order

that was completely destroyed in 70. The Evangelists' reliability in recording these items creates a presumption that their testimony on other matters is reliable also.

5. The Gospels are substantially accurate in reporting the words of Christ.

Although the evangelists in some instances may well have made explicit what was only implicit in the words of Christ when He uttered them, there are many indications that they were concerned to report faithfully the teaching of Christ both in content and in form.

It is an indication of this fidelity as regards content that the theology of the Gospels is much less developed than that of St. Paul, even though they were written after his Epistles. St. Paul, for example, makes much of the redemptive function of the death of Christ, whereas there is only one explicit reference to this in the Gospels (Mk. 10:45).

Again, many of the questions that confronted the early Church, e.g., whether circumcision is necessary for the Christian, could have been answered had it been possible to quote some saying of the Master on the subject, but He had said nothing, and no one dared to invent a saying and attribute it to Him.

The Gospels, moreover, have preserved a number of sayings that do not reflect the attitude of the early Church, e.g., Christ's response to the rich young man: "Why do you call me good? No one is good but God alone" (Mk. 10:18), and his statement that the day and hour of the end of the world are unknown to the Son (Mk. 13:32). These sayings have been recorded because that is what Jesus actually said.

As evidence of their fidelity as regards the form, we have in some instances what Joachim Jeremias calls the very words of Christ, His *ipsissima verba*. Such are the solemn introduction to some of His statements—"Amen, amen, I say to you"; the *'Abba''* with which He addressed the Father; the *"talitha cum"* addressed to the daughter of

Jairus; and the cry on the cross, *"Eloi, Eloi, lama sabach-thani."*

There is further evidence of the fidelity of our texts in reporting the words of Christ that many of them, when translated into Aramaic, the language in which they were spoken, have a rhythmical structure and assonances that would have made them easy to memorize.[33]

In other cases, we have sayings that, if not couched in His exact words are distinctively His *(ipsissima vox).* These, like the parables and passages of the Sermon on the Mount, bear the stamp of His genius and are unique in literature. As the messengers of the Sanhedrin said when they returned to their masters, "No man ever spoke like this man" (Jn. 7:46). The words of Jesus, simple yet profound, often mysterious and paradoxical, have the strange power of speaking individually to every man, of whatever race or time, in language he can understand. As He foretold a few days before His Passion: "Heaven and earth will pass away, but my words will not pass away" (Mk. 13:31).

6. The objectivity of the Gospel narrative.

The Evangelists tell their story objectively, with no expression by their authors of wonderment or sympathy. They report candidly things that were to the discredit of the Apostles—their obtuseness, St. Peter's denial of the Master and their cowardice during the Passion—and this at a time when the Twelve were venerated figures in the Church.

They often report details which could have been omitted without affecting the content of the story and which therefore seem to have been included only because they were in the story as it was told by the original witnesses. Such would be the reference to green grass and groups looking like flower-beds (Mk. 6:39-40), the cushion in the boat (Mk. 4:38), the young man who fled naked from Gethsemane (Mk. 14:51-52), the time of day when the disciples met the Lord (Jn. 1:39), the thirty-eight years' illness of the palsied man (Jn. 5:5) and the one hundred and fifty-three fishes in the morning catch (Jn. 21:11).

"The Gospels," H. E. W. Turner wrote, "give the impression of being honest documents. It has been rightly said that St. Mark never spares the Twelve, and we are left in no doubt of their slowness of heart and unbelief. The story which they tell is the reverse of a success story, and no attempt is made to cloak the decisive rejection of Jesus by those to whom initially He came. There is little attempt to iron out the discrepancies of the tradition, as anyone who has tried to construct a harmony of their narrative quickly comes to realize. Whatever deficiencies a modern historian may ascribe to the Evangelists, lack of honesty is not one of them." [34]

J. B. Phillipps, who devoted many years to the work of translating the New Testament into plain English, testifies in the same vein and thus describes the impression that close study of these documents made on him: "It was the down-to-earth faith of the New Testament writers which conveyed to me that inexpressible sense of the genuine and the authentic.... It is my serious conclusion that we have here in the New Testament, words that bear the hallmark of reality and the ring of truth." [35]

Why, one may ask, are some scholars reluctant to accept the Gospels as reliable accounts of what Christ said and did? Léon-Dufour explains why this should be so. "If the arguments set out in this book are even approximately valid," he writes, "why is there such profound disagreement among scholars on even the trustworthiness of the Gospels? The disagreement ultimately stems, not from dissension over the literary methods employed, but from other presuppositions which have nothing to do with literature. Every man who studies the Gospels either believes that Jesus is the Son of God, or does not believe it, or is on the way to belief or unbelief. Most people who study the Gospel carefully, however, have already made up their minds, before they examine the text, about the possibility or impossibility of supernatural happening in this world." [36]

Non-Christian Sources
of Information About Christ

The events recorded in the New Testament occurred in a period about which we have a great deal of information both from literary sources and from ever-widening archaeological research, even though many of the works of contemporary historians have been lost. Of the works of more than thirty first-century pagan historians, nothing has come down to us.

There are no references to Christ in the few contemporary non-Christian sources that have come down to us, and we have to wait until the end of the first century to find a mention of Him in this literature. This is not surprising, because the life and death of Christ were events of no importance for His pagan contemporaries.

The earliest testimony outside the New Testament is a reference in *The Antiquities of the Jews,* a work by the Jewish writer, *Flavius Josephus,* which appeared in the year 93. The authenticity of the passage has been questioned, but there are good grounds for thinking that some Christian interpolations have been made in a genuine original, so that Josephus can be cited as bearing witness to the existence of Christ.

The Roman historian *Tacitus* has left us in his *Annals,* written about the year 116, a description of Nero's persecution of the Christians after the fire which destroyed much of Rome in 64. These people, he tells us, get their name from one called Christ, who was condemned to be crucified by the procurator Pontius Pilate in the reign of Tiberius.

Another historian, *Suetonius,* writing about the same time as Tacitus, tells us that in the year 49, the Emperor Claudius "expelled the Jews from Rome because, under the influence of one Chrestus, they had become a permanent source of disorder." The most likely cause of this disorder was the conflict between Christian and non-Christian Jews regarding the claims of Christ, Suetonius misinterpreting the story as if Christ was an agitator active in Rome at the time.

Pliny the Younger, during his term as governor of the province of Bithynia in Asia Minor, wrote to the Emperor Trajan in 112, asking him how he was to deal with the Christians in his province, where so many of the citizens had embraced the Christian Faith that the temples of the gods were deserted. He has, he tells Trajan, examined Christians who have been denounced to him, but all that has come to light is that they meet in the morning on fixed days and sing hymns to Christ, invoking Him as a god; that they take an oath not to commit crimes such as theft, adultery and perjury, and gather for a meal in the evenings. In short, he has found nothing evil except superstition, blameworthy because it is a degenerate cult carried to extravagant lengths.

The information we get from these sources is meager, but not without its value as testifying to the impact of Christ on the course of history in the century after His death. Tacitus in particular has information that is accurate and may have been obtained from the imperial archives.

Notes

1. S. Neill, *The Interpretation of the New Testament, 1861-1961,* Oxford University Press, London, 1964, p. 221.

2. Quoted by I. Howard Marshall, *I Believe in the Historical Jesus,* Hodder and Stoughton, London, 1977, p. 12.

3. Article "Reflections d'actualité sur les rechereches exégétiques" in *Revue Thomiste,* Avril-Septembre 1971, pp. 246-279.

4. *Dogmatic Constitution on Divine Revelation,* no. 19.

5. *The Bible and Archaeology.* Quoted by F. F. Bruce, *The New Testament Documents,* Inter-Varsity Press, Leicester, 1976, p. 20.

6. *Memory and Manuscript: Oral Tradition and Written Transmission in Rabbinic Judaism and Early Christianity* (tr. E. J. Sharpe), C. W. K. Gleerup, Uppsala, 1961, p. 328.

7. *The Eternal Son,* Huntington, Indiana, 1978, p. 159.

8. *Ibid.,* p. 155.

9. *Redating the New Testament,* SCM Press, London & Westminster Press, Philadelphia, 1976, p. 358.

10. *The Date of Acts and the Synoptic Gospels* (tr. J. Wilkinson), Williams and Norgate, London, 1911, p. 97.

11. *Ibid.,* p. 99.

12. *Redating,* pp. 89-92.

13. *The Gospels and Acts,* Vol. II, SCM Press, London and Westminster Press, Philadelphia, 1976, p. 247.

14. *Redating,* pp. 102-107.

15. *Ibid.,* p. 101, cf. Chronological Tables, pp. 352-353.

16. *Ibid.,* p. 360.

17. *The Criticism of the Fourth Gospel,* The Clarendon Press, Oxford, 1905, p. 238.

18. *The Character and Authorship of the Fourth Gospel,* Williams and Norgate, London, 1903, p. 348.

19. *The Gospels and Acts,* Vol. II, p. 6.

20. *The Character and Authorship,* p. 369.

21. *Redating,* pp. 309-311.

22. *The Gospels and Acts,* Vol. II, p. 107.

23. *Revue Thomiste,* art. cit.

24. *Redating,* pp. 255-311.

25. *Historical Tradition in the Fourth Gospel,* Cambridge University Press, 1963, p. 423.

26. *Redating,* p. 268.

27. *According to John,* SCM Press, London, 1869, pp. 56-65.

28. *Ibid.,* pp. 90-101.

29. *The Man Born To Be King,* Victor Gollancz, London, 1943, p. 33.

30. *A Lawyer Among the Theologians,* Hodder and Stoughton, London, 1973, p. 35.

31. Quoted in Anderson, *op. cit.,* p. 38.

32. *The Gospels and the Jesus of History* (tr. John McHugh), Collins, London, 1968, p. 164.

33. Joachim Jeremias, *New Testament Theology,* Vol. 1, SCM Press, London, and Charles Scribners Son, New York, 1973, pp. 3-29.

34. Quoted in Anderson, *op. cit.,* p. 40.

35. *The Ring of Truth,* Hodder and Stoughton, London, 1967, pp. 95-96.

36. *The Gospels and the Jesus of History,* p. 271.

References

N. Anderson, *A Lawyer Among the Theologians,* Hodder and Stoughton, London, 1973. A distinguished lawyer comments adversely on the logic of the biblical scholars.

W. Barclay, *The Gospels and Acts,* 2 Volumes, Hodder and Stoughton, London, 1976. A very thorough, clear and fair account of such topics as the Synoptic Problem, the development of modern biblical criticism, the date and authorship of the four Gospels and the Acts.

L. Bouyer, *The Eternal Son,* Our Sunday Visitor, Huntington, Indiana, 1978. Probably the best recent work on Christology, by a scholar who is well informed on developments in biblical studies and speculative theology.

F. F. Bruce, *The New Testament Documents: Are They Reliable?* Inter-Varsity Press, Leicester, 1960. A brief (120 pp.) but valuable defense of the New Testament documents by the Rylands Professor of Biblical Criticism and Exegesis in the University of Manchester.

C. H. Dodd, *Historical Tradition in the Fourth Gospel,* Cambridge University Press, Cambridge, 1963. In this epoch-making work, Dodd develops a thesis put forward by Gardner-Smith in 1935.

J. Drummond, *The Character and Authorship of the Fourth Gospel,* Williams and Norgate, London, 1903. A comprehensive study of the Gospel by a Unitarian. Drummond deals at length with the objections raised against the Johannine authorship. Still well worth reading.

A. C. Headlam, *The Fourth Gospel as History,* Blackwell, Oxford, 1948. A hard-hitting defense of the historical worth of the Fourth Gospel by the former bishop of Gloucester.

E. Hoskyns and N. Davey, *The Riddle of the New Testament,* Faber and Faber, London, 1931. A valuable survey of the results of historical criticism of the New Testament, showing how Christ's claims are unique.

A. M. Hunter, *According to John,* SCM Press, London, 1968. A concise (118 pp.) account of the fruits of recent research by the Professor Emeritus of New Testament in the University of Aberdeen. Probably the best introduction of the Fourth Gospel for the general reader.

R. Latourelle, S.J., *Finding Jesus Through the Gospels* (E. T. A. Owen), Alba House, New York, 1979. The author, Professor of Fundamental Theology in the Gregorian University, Rome, discusses the possibility of historically finding Jesus through the Gospels, and provides a critical, positive answer.

X. Léon-Dufour, S.J., *The Gospels and the Jesus of History* (tr. J. McHugh), Collins, London, 1968. The author, Professor of Scripture in Fourviere-Lyon, argues that the Gospels contain a wealth of trustworthy historical information about Jesus.

L. Marshall, *I Believe in the Historical Jesus,* Hodder and Stoughton, London, 1977. The author, Senior Lecturer in New Testament Exegesis in the University of Aberdeen, discusses the relation of history to faith, and after examining the evidence concludes that the Gospels provide reliable historical information about Jesus.

Luke, Historian and Theologian, Paternostic Press, Exeter, 1970. Marshall argues that Luke is not only a theologian but also a reliable historian.

E. L. Mascall, *The Secularization of Christianity,* Darton, Longman and Todd, London, 1965. In the final chapter of this book, entitled "Fact and the Gospels," Mascall, a well-known theologian, effectively refutes several scholars who are sceptical of the historical worth of the New Testament documents.

Leon Morris, *Studies in the Fourth Gospel,* Eerdmans, Grand Rapids, 1969. In this book, Morris, a conservative scholar of international reputation, states the case for the Johannine authorship of the Gospel and its claim to be the account of an eye-witness.

C. F. D. Moule, *The Birth of the New Testament,* third edition, A. and C. Black, London, 1981. An excellent study by a conservative Anglican scholar.

S. Neill, *The Interpretation of the New Testament 1861-1961,* Oxford University Press, London, 1964. An excellent critical survey of New Testament scholarship in the century under review.

James T. O'Connor, *The Father's Son,* St. Paul Editions, Boston, 1984. An excellent study, scholarly and orthodox, of the New Testament witness to our Lord.

J. A. T. Robinson, *Redating the New Testament,* SCM Press, London, 1976. Though few will accept the author's contention that *all* the New Testament books were written before 70, he has succeeded in establishing an early date for several that are usually dated later. Robinson is a first rate New Testament scholar, and most informative even if he sometimes fails to convince.

Can We Trust the New Testament? A. R. Mowbray, London, 1977. This paperback (134 pp.) summarizes some of the arguments in *Redating,* and answers the question in the title in the affirmative.

W. Sanday, *The Criticism of the Fourth Gospel,* Clarendon Press, Oxford, 1905. A classical statement of the case for the Johannine authorship by the Lady Margaret Professor of Divinity at Oxford. Still well worth reading.

H. E. W. Turner, *Jesus, Master and Lord,* A. R. Mowbray, London, 1953. The sub-title of this book by the Lightfoot Professor of Divinity in the University of Durham is "A Study in the Historical Truth of the Gospels." It shows how the evidence the Gospels provide is in line with the historical faith of the Church regarding the Person of the Master.

V. The Witness of Jesus Regarding Himself

John the Baptist, the last of the prophets, began to preach in the wilderness of Judah, probably in 27 A.D. His message was: "Repent, for the kingdom of God is at hand." When the Jews, thinking John might be the long-awaited Messiah, asked him if he were, he answered that he was not. He was, he said, only the herald, "a voice crying in the wilderness," a forerunner, preparing the way for Another, greater than he, whose sandals he was not worthy to carry.

Jesus, making His way to the Jordan, was baptized by John and then went into the wilderness for forty days. Returning to the Jordan, He was joined by Andrew and John—who until then had been disciples of John the Baptist—and a little later by Simon, Philip and Nathanael. Some time later, moving north, He began the Galilean phase of His ministry, making Capernaum, a lakeside town, His headquarters. The theme of His preaching was: "The time is fulfilled, and the kingdom of God is at hand; repent, and believe in the gospel" (Mk. 1:15). Throughout the Galilean ministry the central theme of Jesus' preaching was the coming reign of God. In numerous parables He described its origin, its development, and its consummation, set out the conditions which must be fulfilled by those who would become God's subjects in His kingdom, and stressed the need for prompt acceptance of the invitation to enter the kingdom.

A Hiatus?

At first glance this preaching of Christ in Galilee seems very different from that of the Apostles after Pentecost. Whereas He spoke of the coming of the kingdom of God, the central theme of their preaching was Christ Himself. Thus St. Peter, whether he was addressing a crowd at Pentecost (Acts 2) or the members of the Sanhedrin (Acts 4), was intent on proclaiming that Jesus, who had been crucified, had risen from the dead, fulfilling the Old Testament prophecies and thereby proving that He was the expected Messiah in whom all men were called to believe.

Similarly, St. Paul declared that his preaching was centered on Christ:

"Jews demand signs and Greeks seek wisdom, but we preach Christ crucified, a stumbling block to Jews and folly to Gentiles, but to those who are called, both Jews and Greeks, Christ the power of God and the wisdom of God" (1 Cor. 1:22-24).

Some scholars have held that we have here a hiatus, that the preaching of the Apostles marks a radical departure from the teaching of Jesus. Harnack, for example, held that Jesus had no place in His own Gospel, for His only concern was to proclaim the Fatherhood of God and the infinite value of the human soul. Thus there would have been nothing about Christ Himself in the Gospel of Christ. Harnack did, however, admit that at some point Jesus realized that He was the Messiah, but this was not the main point of His preaching. Wrede went much further than Harnack and declared that the life of Jesus was not Messianic and that He never claimed to be the Messiah. Bultmann said he doubted whether Jesus made any Messianic claim at all.

Not many scholars share this scepticism. Most now agree that Jesus regarded Himself as the Messiah, and many hold that the Apostolic preaching about Christ has its source in the revelation, guarded at first, which He made of Himself during His public ministry. "Is it likely," asks Stephen Neill, "that the believers came to this understand-

ing of the centrality of Jesus for faith, but that Jesus Himself was unaware of His own significance in the purpose of
God?"[1]

Oscar Cullmann answers the question with a categorical *no*. "All Christology," he writes, "is founded upon the
life of Jesus. Although this assertion appears to be a truism,
yet it must be emphasized—and not only against those
who question Jesus' historical existence. The question
'Who is Jesus?' did not emerge for the first time with the
early community's experience of Easter. The life of Jesus
already provided the starting point of all Christological
thought in a double way: in Jesus' own self-consciousness
and in the concrete presentiment His person and work
evoked among the disciples and the people."[2]

There has been no real hiatus, but only a process of
development.

All that happened was that the centrality of Christ,
which was implicit in His preaching of the kingdom of
God in Galilee became explicit in the preaching of the
Apostles after the Resurrection. Moreover, as T. W. Manson
has pointed out, this had already been preceded by a
development in the preaching of Christ Himself. "The
decisive point," he writes, "is Peter's declaration: 'Thou
are the Christ.' From this point onwards the life and teaching both move in a new direction. A regular feature of the
speech of Jesus before this point is a demand for insight
and understanding on the part of His hearers. This is now
replaced by a demand for loyalty and endurance on the
part of His followers...."[3]

What the Apostles did was to take this revelation one
stage further, making Christ Himself the center of their
preaching. Why this took place has been well explained by
P. T. Forsyth: "The Gospel of Christ replaced the Gospel of
the kingdom because by His death He became the kingdom, because He became all that the kingdom contained.... The testimony of Jesus is the Spirit of the
kingdom. The Gospel of the kingdom was Christ in essence; Christ was the Gospel of the kingdom in power.
The kingdom was Christ in a mystery; Christ was the

publication, the establishment of the kingdom.... He was the truth of His own greatest Gospel. It is whatever He is. To have Him is to ensure it."[4]

The Messiah

Jesus' revelation of Himself as the long-awaited Messiah was an essential element in the good news He proclaimed. But in making this revelation He had to exercise great reserve, since His conception of His Messianic role differed widely from that of His contemporaries, including the Apostles (cf. Acts 1:6).

It is clear from the Gospels (e.g., John 6:15) that many Jews at that time were thinking of the Messiah as a great king who would establish a world-wide empire with Jerusalem as its capital. It would be at the same time a spiritual kingdom, in which the God of Israel would be worshiped, and an earthly kingdom, ushering in an era of peace and prosperity for all mankind. Under this scheme of things, the immediate task of the Messiah would be to restore independence to Israel, freeing her from the hated Roman yoke and making her a great nation. Under the circumstances this political Messianism was an explosive creed, for the Romans had no intention of granting Israel her independence, a point they had made in 6 A.D., when they ruthlessly suppressed a Messianic insurrection led by Judas the Galilean, razing the town of Sepphoris to the ground.

Since Jesus' mission was essentially spiritual, He could not afford to let it be compromised by being exploited for political ends. So, although He never rejected the title of Messiah as John the Baptist had done (John 1:20), He gave no encouragement to those who in their enthusiasm were making this claim for Him. He urged the beneficiaries of His miracles to say nothing about them, and when the crowd, impressed by His feeding of the five thousand, wanted to make Him king, He fled into the hills and shortly afterwards concluded His preaching in Galilee.

It is in the Gospel of St. Mark especially that Jesus' reticence about His Messianic role is stressed, and some

have contended that Mark has made too much of the
"Messianic secret." But there is good evidence that Mark's
account of the matter is substantially correct; as we have
said, the circumstances called for great reticence on the
part of Jesus.

This reticence, however, did not prevent Him from
indicating early in His ministry that with His coming the
Messianic age had begun. In the synagogue at Nazareth,
after reading the prophetic passage from Isaiah 61, He
declared: "Today this scripture has been fulfilled in your
hearing" (Lk. 4:21).

Similarly, when the Baptist sent messengers to Jesus to
ask: "Are you he who is to come, or shall we look for
another?" He replied by appealing to His miracles as the
fulfillment of the Old Testament prophecies (Mt. 11:2-6; cf.
Is. 35:5-6; 61:1).

Where there was no danger of political repercussions,
as when He was talking to the woman at Jacob's well (Jn.
4:26), He did reveal that He was the Messiah. He accepted
Peter's expression of faith in Him as the Messiah, but
forbade His disciples to speak of this to anyone (Mk.
8:29-30). His triumphant entry into Jerusalem in circumstances recalling the prophecy of Zechariah (9:9), looks
uncommonly like a Messianic gesture or demonstration,
but so staged as if to say, "If I am the Messiah, I am not
going to fight the Romans, but to fight abuse at the heart
of Judaism." And finally, when it is perfectly clear that no
violent action is possible, because He is already a prisoner,
He acknowledges before the Sanhedrin that He is the
Messiah (Mk. 14:62).[5]

That Jesus was the Messiah, the Christ, was from the
first the burden of the apostolic preaching (cf. Acts 2:37).
The title was in fact so much His that it became transformed from a common into a proper name "Jesus Christ"
(cf. Rom. 1:1). Between the faith of the early Church and
the consciousness of Jesus there is not a radical break, but
continuity. "The early Church," Cullmann wrote, "believed in Christ's messiahship only because it believed that
Jesus believed Himself to be Messiah."[6]

The Son of Man

Although some scholars (e.g., Bornkamm) have held the contrary view, it is certain that Jesus spoke of Himself as "the Son of Man." In the Gospels, the phrase is found only on His lips, and in the rest of the New Testament only in two places—the speech of Stephen before the Sanhedrin (Acts 7:56) and in the Apocalypse (1:13; 14:14). In both these passages, it may be noted, it is a question of vision, a vision which harks back to the vision recorded in the book of Daniel (7:13).

"It is remarkable," Joachim Jeremias writes, "that in all four Gospels the title occurs *exclusively* on the lips of Jesus. Here the tradition is quite consistent. The title Son of Man does not occur in any confessional formula of the early Church.

"Nowhere in the Gospel account is Jesus designated as Son of Man, nor is He addressed as Son of Man in prayer. There is not a single passage in the Gospels in which the title is used in statements about Jesus. On the contrary, it is firmly anchored in the sayings of Jesus." What is the explanation? Jeremias answers, "There can only be one answer; the title was rooted in the tradition of the sayings of Jesus right from the beginning; as a result it was sacrosanct, and no one dared to eliminate it."[7]

"The Son of Man" is an enigmatic phrase, intended to give rise to questioning in the minds of those who heard it. So the Jews were moved to ask the question: "How can you say that the Son of Man must be lifted up? Who is this Son of Man?" (Jn. 12:34)

Moule comments on the fact that in the Gospels this phrase always has the definite article. He writes: "I am among those who still believe that it is Daniel (ch. 7) that gives the phrase, in the Gospel tradition, its decisive color. And what confirms me in this conclusion is, among other things, the fact that almost invariably in the Gospel tradition the phrase is not in fact 'Son of Man,' but *'the* Son of Man,' with the definite article. This leads me to believe that what lies behind the Greek, *Ho huios tou anthropou,* must be some Aramaic expression that meant, unequivocally, not just 'Son of Man' but *'the* Son of Man' or *that* Son of Man, and that this phrase was thus demonstrative because it expressly referred to Daniel's Son of Man."[8]

Ignoring the few dissentient voices, Léon-Dufour writes: "All modern writers agree that Jesus Himself used the title in the sense it has in Daniel, where it denotes a heavenly being who brings salvation and who embodies in Himself the kingdom of the saints of the Most High (Dan. 7:13).... In calling Himself by this title, Jesus implicitly claimed a heavenly origin and the role of judge at the end of time; He also said that He had come to inaugurate the Messianic era (Mt. 12:8) and to save sinners (Mt. 9:6); but He toned down the glorious character of the Son of Man by insisting that He who would judge mankind at the end of history was, here now, a Servant come to suffer and die for the love of mankind (cf. Isaiah 53)."[9]

H. E. W. Turner also makes the point that the phrase as it was used by Jesus alludes to the two aspects of His Messianic mission, His humiliation and His exaltation, and was very suitable as containing at once the Messianic claim and an indication that it was not in accord with Jewish preconceptions. He writes: "It interprets the claim to be Messiah both in terms of the supernatural heavenly being of the apocalyptic tradition and of the Suffering Servant of prophecy. It holds together two contrasted but necessary aspects of the Messiahship of Jesus: His humiliation and His exaltation. Its use may well be associated with the Messianic cross-purposes which we have seen evidenced between Jesus and His contemporaries, and the relative indirectness of Messianic claim which it appears to have necessitated. Perhaps we may make bold to say that no term could have been better suited to tell us so much of what He conceived Himself to be with so little of the dangerously false associations which belonged to other terms which embodied the hope of the Jewish people of intervention of God through a Messianic figure. If, as we believe, it was part of the intention of Jesus to take old terms and to fill them with a new and characteristic content, such a procedure would have been in complete harmony with what we can still today discover of His mind." [10]

The Suffering Servant

"The Son of Man" was a term of glory with which Jesus described His future royal status. But He made it clear that the path to glory was to be one of suffering, as He stated emphatically after Peter had acknowledged Him as the Messiah at Caesarea Philippi (Mk. 8:31-33).

Jesus saw His Messianic mission as the fulfillment of the prophecy of Isaiah 53 that God would redeem His people from their sins by the sufferings of His faithful servant. As is clear from Peter's reaction to the prophecy of the Passion (Mk. 8:32), this was a new and startling development in the concept of the Messiah. As Cullmann says, "One can at best find faint traces of a suffering Messiah in Judaism." [11]

It is not clear whether the passages of Isaiah concerning the Servant of the Lord refer to an individual personality or a collective one, such as would be the "faithful remnant" of the people. By applying the prophecy to Himself, Jesus solves the problem—He, suffering alone on the cross, is the faithful remnant of the people.

"The passages in Isaiah referring to the Servant of the Lord (42:1-4; 49:1-6; 50:4-11; 52:13-53)," H. E. W. Turner writes, "are most probably to be interpreted in the light of the concept of corporate personality to which reference has already been made. The background is the rather flexible concept of the relation between the individual and the community which made it possible for the thought of many Hebrew writers to pass from the individual to the group and the group to the individual without any feeling of strain. Perhaps the most probable interpretation of the Songs is that the prophet begins by reflecting upon the fortunes of his people, then passes to think of the people as the righteous remnant or spiritual nucleus among them, and finally envisages such a mission and destiny for this righteous remnant as passing wholly beyond what was possible for a body of people, and reaches a description of the Servant which could only find fulfillment in an individual and in a unique Individual at that. It is perhaps easier for us to trace a development in the writer's thought than it was for the writer himself, because our thought is not so much colored by the concept of corporate personality, and partly because we stand on the other side of the fact of Christ and can see not only what it was possible for the Jewish people to achieve, but also what God has actually done in Christ." [12]

On three occasions Jesus foretold His Passion (Mk. 8:31; 9:31; 10:33-34), but these passages form only a small part of the comprehensive amount of material which deals with His future suffering. This is referred to in the passage in which He speaks of the punishment in store for the murderers of God's messengers (Mt. 23:34-36), in the accusation He brings against Jerusalem which murders the prophets (Mt. 23:37-39) and is preparing to murder the heir (Mk. 12:8).

There can be no doubt that Jesus saw that His conflict with the Jewish authorities over such matters as the observance of the Sabbath would lead eventually to His death. But not only did He foresee His death, He also saw it as making atonement for the sins of men. This is clear from His words: "The Son of Man also came not to be served but to serve, and to give his life as a ransom for many" (Mk. 10:45). The phrase "for many" is inclusive (i.e., "many" means "all"), and it certainly harks back to the words of Isaiah: "By his knowledge shall the righteous one, my servant, make many to be accounted righteous; and he shall bear their iniquities...because he poured out his soul to death, and was numbered with the transgressors; yet he bore the sin of many, and made intercession for the transgressors" (53:11-12).

There is also a reference to this passage in Isaiah in the words with which Jesus instituted the Eucharist: "This is my blood of the covenant, which is poured out for many" (Mk. 14:24). Nor can there be much doubt that He had in mind the words of Isaiah, "He was despised and rejected

by men" (53:3), when He said: It is "written of the Son of
Man that he should suffer many things and be treated with
contempt" (Mk. 9:12).

That Christ died to atone for sin was an essential
element of the Apostolic preaching from the beginning, as
we see from the very early formula which St. Paul quotes
in writing to the Corinthians: "For I delivered to you as of
first importance what I also received, that Christ died for
our sins in accordance with the scriptures" (1 Cor. 15:3).
As we might expect, there are many references to this
teaching elsewhere in the New Testament (cf. Rom. 4:25;
1 Pt. 2:24; Heb. 9:26-28).

In the Gospels, on the other hand, there are few
references to the expiatory character of Christ's sufferings
and death. The reason for this, as Joachim Jeremias points
out,[13] is that Christ spoke of this deepest secret of His
mission only when instructing His disciples, and even then
only in the last period of His ministry. He could attribute
atoning power to His death because He died as the Servant
of God whose suffering and death had been foretold by
Isaiah. His suffering and death has the same characteristics:
it is innocent (53:9), it is voluntary (v. 10), patiently borne
(v. 7), willed by God (vvs. 6, 10), and therefore atoning for
many (vvs. 4ff.). Moreover, His death has unlimited power
to atone for sin because it is the death of the Son of God.

The Son of God

This title is applied to Christ by St. Mark at the beginning of his Gospel, and he records its use by the demoni-
acs (3:11; 5:7), the high priest (14:61) and the centurion at
the Crucifixion (15:39). St. Mark's witness to Christ is
sometimes interpreted as if it so concentrates on His humanity as to leave His divinity in the background, thereby
providing the basis for the "Christology from below"
which has recently become fashionable in some circles.
This, as Vincent Taylor has pointed out, is a misinterpretation of the Gospel of St. Mark. He writes: "The sheer
humanity of the Markan portraiture catches the eye of the

most careless reader; and yet it is but half seen if it is not perceived that this Man of Sorrows is also a Being of supernatural origin and dignity, since He is the Son of God. The same conception lies behind the use of the title Son of Man, for He is not only the Suffering Servant, but also the one who will sit at God's right hand and come with power upon the clouds of heaven (14:62). Mark's Christology is a high Christology, as high as any in the New Testament, not excluding that of John." [14]

When Joseph and Mary found the child Jesus in the Temple, He said to them: "Did you not know that I must be in my Father's house?" (Lk. 2:49) The question implies that He enjoys a special relationship with the Father to whom He here, as always, refers as *"my* Father."

The parable of the wicked husbandmen (Mk. 12:1-9), as the Jewish leaders understood, was concerned with the present situation: "They perceived that he had told the parable against them" (Mk. 12:12). In the parable those whom the owner of the vineyard sends to collect the fruits of the vineyard and whom the tenants treat shamefully, beating some and killing others, are the prophets. Jesus, who comes last of all, comes not as a servant but as the Son, the "beloved Son" of the Father, and indeed His heir—all that belongs to the Father will by right of inheritance be His. This claim to a transcendent position in the divine plan, made shortly before the Passion, was surely one of the factors that prompted the high priest in the trial before the Sanhedrin to issue the solemn challenge that sealed Jesus' fate: "Are you the Christ, the Son of the Blessed?" (Mk. 14:61)

It has often been remarked that the second stanza of the "Great Thanksgiving" which Jesus uttered when the disciples returned from their successful mission reads like a passage from the Gospel of St. John: "All things have been delivered to me by my Father; and no one knows the Son except the Father, and no one knows the Father except the Son and any one to whom the Son chooses to reveal him" (Mt. 11:27). In these words, Jesus claims not only that He is the organ of God's self-revelation, but that

He alone knows God truly as Father, and all who come to share in that knowledge are indebted to Him. His sonship is "unshared sonship"—a filial relationship with the Father, for which there is no parallel anywhere else and which is the secret of His ministry and His work.

It is certain that Jesus always spoke of God as "my Father," whereas for those to whom He spoke God was "your Father," whom they were to address in prayer as "our Father." This usage is constant in the words of Christ, and the implication is clear—His relationship with the Father is unique, of a different order from that which His disciples enjoy. That Jesus should have spoken of God as "my Father" was quite unusual. It was even more unusual that He should have addressed Him as *Abba*. To His contemporaries it would have seemed disrespectful, even unthinkable, that anyone should address God with this familiar word, used by sons and daughters in the family circle. The uniqueness of *Abba* as the term by which Jesus addressed the Father in His prayer, Joachim Jeremias writes, expresses the heart of His relationship with the Father and the ultimate mystery of His mission.[15]

The Witness of the Miracles

Jesus revealed who He was, not only by describing Himself as "the Son of Man" or "the Son," but also by the miracles He worked and the manner in which He worked them.

The primary purpose of the miracles was to reveal who He was and the nature of His mission.

He casts out devils by His own authority, ordering them to depart from the persons of whom they had taken possession (Mk. 1:23-27).

He heals the paralytic to prove that He has the power to forgive sin. For the scribes who were looking on, this claim was equivalent to blasphemy, since only God can forgive sin (Mk. 2:3-12).

He cures the man with a withered hand as a sign that justifies His claim to be Lord of the Sabbath, the day of the Lord (Mk. 2:28—3:5).

In an acted parable, He curses the barren fig-tree, to signify the rejection of Israel (Mk. 11:14, 20). In the parable of the barren fig-tree in the Gospel of St. Luke there is the same message regarding the fate that awaits Israel if she refuses to repent and believe in Him (13:6-9).

With a word of command Jesus cures the leper (Mk. 1:41), raises the dead to life (Mk. 5:41-42) and stills the storm at sea (Mk. 4:41). "Who is this," the Apostles asked, "that even wind and sea obey him?" (Mk. 4:41) We too may ask a similar question: "Who then is this, who has authority to deprive Satan of his retinue of human slaves, to forgive sin and to reject the people of Israel?"

The Witness of the Parables

The parables of Jesus are much more than similitudes or stories used to illustrate some spiritual or moral truth. As C. H. Dodd and Joachim Jeremias have shown, all the parables have to do—in one way or another—with the coming of the kingdom of God. This phrase "the kingdom of God" signifies the reign or sovereignty of God in action and the new order of things which the action of God is to establish. For centuries the Jews had been praying for the time when God would manifest His great power and reign. The "good news" that Jesus brought was that the kingdom of God was near at hand: "The time is fulfilled, and the kingdom of God is at hand" (Mk. 1:15). This is the background of the parables—the great campaign of the kingdom of God, with Jesus as its spearhead, against the kingdom of the Evil One.

If then we are to understand the parables aright we must see them in their historical setting as words spoken by Jesus in vindication of His Messianic mission. Thus the parables of the Mustard Seed and the Leaven describe the growth and abiding influence of the apparently insignificant group consisting of Himself and His handful of followers. The parable of the Laborers in the Vineyard is His reply to the Pharisees who were criticizing Him for offering the blessings of the kingdom to tax-collectors and sinners. The parables of the Lost Sheep, the Lost Coin and the Prodigal Son, in telling of God's desire to save His lost children, are in effect a justification of the policy which He, as God's Envoy, has been following in seeking to heal those who were spiritually sick.

To enter the kingdom is to become a disciple of Jesus. But He who would become a disciple of Jesus must sit down and reckon the cost, like the man who would build a tower or the king who is thinking of waging war (Lk. 14:27-33). And the parable of the Two Builders with which He ends the Sermon on the Mount contrasts the fate of those who hear His words and live by them—His true disciples—with those who hear them and refuse to live by them—like the Pharisees.

Finally there are the parables He spoke as the great drama moved to its climax, the great crisis which would involve not only the Messiah's death and victory and the rise of a new Israel, but also the Jewish nation and its Temple. The only one that is directly Christological is that of the Wicked Vinedressers which we have discussed already. In such others as the Waiting Servants, the Ten Bridesmaids, and the Unjust Steward, He is warning His hearers not to be unprepared in the approaching crisis, God's time of destiny for His chosen people. There is yet time to accept Him as their Messiah. If they fail to do so, their fate is sealed.

In His parables, and especially those He uttered on the way to make His final challenge in Jerusalem, we see Jesus as the central figure and precipitant of the great crisis which culminated in the cross and all that followed it, saying things which none short of the Messiah had the right to say and knowing Himself to be the sole bearer of Israel's destiny. So that at the last, when He hung on the cross, He was in very truth Israel Himself (as He had claimed to be in the Upper Room when He said "I am the true vine" [Jn. 15:1], the heavenly Vine of which the vine brought out of Egypt [Ps. 80(79):8-16] was but the earthly shadow).

"In studying the parables," A. M. Hunter writes, "we ought, therefore, keep our ears open for this note of sovereign authority; for the parables no less than the cross pose the problem of Christ's person. They impel us to ask: Who can this be in whom God's kingdom, His saving sovereignty, is centered, who knows Himself to be the decisive person in God's ways with Israel and, through Israel, the wider world?"[16]

Christ's Astounding Claims

There are many passages in the Gospels where Christ lays claim to prerogatives which far outstrip those which could rightly be claimed by any merely human emissary from God.

He demands complete devotion to Himself, so that if there is conflict with family ties, even the closest of these must be sacrificed: "He who loves father or mother more than me is not worthy of me; and he who loves son or daughter more than me is not worthy of me" (Mt. 10:37).

He declares that a man's final destiny will be determined by His readiness to proclaim His faith in Christ: "Every one who acknowledges me before men, I also will acknowledge before my Father who is in heaven; but whoever denies me before men, I also will deny before my Father who is in heaven" (Mt. 10:32-33).

He identifies His cause with the cause of God: "He who receives you receives me, and he who receives me receives him who sent me" (Mt. 10:40).

It has been said that Jesus never asked men to believe in Him, but only in the Father. This is quite false. When He said "Follow me," "Learn of me," "Come to me," "Forsake all and follow me," He was demanding faith in Himself no less insistently than the Apostles would demand faith in Him later on.

When He said to the woman who was a sinner: "Your faith has saved you; go in peace" (Lk. 7:50), He clearly implied that it was faith in Him that had won for her forgiveness of her sins.

"Jesus' view of His status," Joachim Jeremias writes, "is expressed even more clearly...in the remarkable accumulation of the emphatic *ego* in His sayings, to the same degree in both the synoptic and Johannine material. It is to be found not only in sayings of Jesus about His mission like Matthew 5:17, but also throughout His preaching"[17]

There is a striking example of this in the Sermon on the Mount (Mt. 5:21-48) where Jesus contrasts His teaching on six points with that of the Old Testament: "You have heard that it was said to the men of old...but I say to you...."

Moses and the prophets came as messengers of the Lord and demanded acceptance of their message because it was guaranteed by His authority: "Thus says the Lord."

Jesus, on the other hand, lays down the law on His own authority, and on the question of divorce, He overrides the law of Moses, abolishing the permission which Moses had granted to the Jews "because of the hardness of their hearts."

We find the same emphatic "I" in such passages as these: "Behold, *I* send you out as sheep in the midst of wolves" (Mt. 10:16).

"If it is by the Spirit of God that *I* cast out demons..." (Mt. 12:28).

"Come to *me,* all who labor and are heavy laden, and *I* will give you rest" (Mt. 11:28).

"*I* have come not to abolish [the law and the prophets] but to fulfill them" (Mt. 5:17).

"*I* came not to call the righteous, but sinners" (Mk. 2:17).

"*I* have not come to bring peace, but a sword" (Mt. 10:34).

"*I* came to cast fire upon the earth..." (Lk. 12:49).

The emphatic *ego,* so prominent in the Synoptic Gospels, is even more prominent in the Gospel of St. John, e.g., "*I* am the bread of life" (6:35), "*I* am the good shepherd" (10:14), and here, as in the Synoptics, is an indication of Jesus' awareness of His unique status in the divine plan of salvation.

Christ's Witness to Himself in the Gospel of St. John

So far we have confined our attention almost entirely to material found in the Synoptic Gospels. When we turn to the Gospel of St. John we find Christ affirming His Godhead in language that is clearer than anything to be found in the Synoptic Gospels.

The force of these words has been discounted as though St. John were a less reliable witness than the Synoptic writers, but scepticism about His reliability has for some time been declining.

He differs from the Synoptics in this, that He makes explicit in the testimony of Jesus what they leave implicit. Nevertheless, there are many points at which His witness coincides with theirs. A. M. Hunter has drawn attention to more than two dozen synoptic-like sayings in St. John's Gospel and C. H. Dodd has laid bare half a dozen dialogues which are the counterpart of similar dialogues in the Synoptics.[18]

The controversies with the Jewish leaders (chs. 7, 8, 10) have no parallel in the Synoptic Gospels, but this is accounted for partly by the fact that the Synoptics tell us very little about the last months of Jesus' life, and partly by the difference of audience—Galilean peasants on the one hand and learned rabbis on the other. We have already quoted the testimony of Israel Abrahams that Jewish writers favor the authenticity of these discourses reported in the Fourth Gospel.

In chapter 8 of the Gospel we have the record of a debate with the Pharisees. Jesus made the claim: "I am the light of the world." The Pharisees rejected this claim as untrue. Jesus pointed out that the claim was supported by the testimony of His Father, and so, since the testimony of two witnesses sufficed to guarantee the truth of a statement, the claim was true. If anyone accepted the witness of Him who was the light of the world, he would know the truth, and this knowledge would make Him free. The Pharisees retorted that because they were the children of Abraham, they were already free. After some debate regarding their descent from Abraham, Jesus went on to speak of His relationship to Abraham. "Abraham," He said, "rejoiced that he was to see my day; he saw it and was glad." At once the Jews objected, "You are not yet fifty years old, and have you seen Abraham?" Jesus met the question with the startling statement, "Truly, truly, I say to you, before Abraham was, I am." On hearing these words which they took as blasphemy, His adversaries took up stones to throw at Him. A similar incident is recorded in Chapter 10. There Jesus declares that He is the Good Shepherd, implying that in Him is fulfilled the word God spoke by the mouth of Ezekiel: "I myself will be the shepherd of my sheep, and I will make them lie down, says the Lord God" (34:15). He then goes on to say that, just as no one can snatch the sheep out of the Father's hand, so no one can snatch them out of His hand, for He and the Father are one. His hearers met this claim with the charge of blasphemy and made ready to stone Him. To justify His claim, Jesus appealed to the text in which the psalmist addressed judges as "gods" (82[81]:6). His argument is *a fortiori:* if Scripture applies the name "gods" to judges commissioned to act in God's name, it is unreasonable to accuse God's consecrated ambassador of blasphemy because He calls Himself God's Son. Addressed to rabbis, it is a rabbinical argument, put forward by Jesus to justify His claim to possess a special relationship with the Father, without attempting to settle the exact nature of this relationship.

At the Last Supper, when He could speak more freely than ever before, Jesus revealed in the clearest terms His unity with the Father. The disciples were to believe in Him, as they believed in the Father (Jn. 14:1); seeing Him, they saw the Father, for He was in the Father and the Father in Him (14:9-10); what they ask for in His name, the Father will grant (16:23), or Jesus Himself will grant (14:14).

There is no need to labor the point, for there has never been any question that the Jesus of the Gospel of St. John claimed to possess the same divine nature as the Father: "All that the Father has is mine" (16:15).

The Trial Before the Sanhedrin

Fifty years ago Lietzmann argued that the Gospel accounts of a trial by the Sanhedrin are a romance without any foundation in fact, and his view has been adopted by such writers as Bornkamm[19] and Senior.[20] As Sherwin-White has shown[21] there is no ground for these doubts, for the Gospel record fits in well with what we know from other sources of Jewish and Roman legal procedures at the time.

Meeting at night, the Sanhedrin sentenced Jesus to death for blasphemy, but had to have its sentence ratified by Pilate, because it had not the right to inflict capital punishment, this right being strictly reserved to the Roman procurator. That this was the Roman policy is certain, even though Stephen was stoned a few years later and James was put to death probably during an interregnum.

After being questioned by Annas regarding His teaching and His disciples, Jesus was led to Caiaphas, the high priest at the time (Annas having been deposed earlier by the Romans), to be tried by the Sanhedrin. When the charge of threatening to destroy the Temple broke down because the witnesses for the prosecution gave conflicting evidence, Caiaphas brought the issue to a head by asking Jesus to say who He was: "Are you the Christ, the Son of the Blessed?" To this Jesus replied: "I am; and you will see the Son of Man sitting at the right hand of Power, and coming with the clouds of heaven." On hearing these words, the high priest tore his mantle, and said: "'Why do we still need witnesses? You have heard his blasphemy. What is your decision?' And they all condemned him as deserving death" (Mk. 14:61-64).

In the other Synoptic Gospels (Mt. 26:64; Lk. 22:70), Christ's reply to the question put to Him by the high priest is less categorical: "You say that I am," but He confirms the suspicions of His questioner by declaring that as the Son of Man He will be seated at the right hand of God.

The claim to be the Messiah was not blasphemous. "There is not one single instance," Bornkamm writes, "of a person's ever being accused of blasphemy and sentenced to death by the Jewish authorities because He claimed to be the Messiah."[22] The blasphemy for which Jesus was condemned lay in making a claim which incorporated all the claims, implicit and explicit, which the Jewish leaders had found so offensive during the previous three years, notably that of having the right to override the traditional interpretations of the Sabbath law. Now He had spoken openly and made His claim to be the Son of God in a unique sense, a claim which the Sanhedrin could not but regard as blasphemous and deserving of the death penalty. So, when it seemed that Pilate might discharge the prisoner as not guilty of the political charges brought against Him, the Jewish leaders fell back on the religious charge: "We have a law, and by that law he ought to die, because he has made himself the Son of God" (Jn. 19:7). This charge Pilate finally accepted under the sort of political pressure that is indicated, in a convincing technicality, by St. John: "If you release this man, you are not Caesar's friend" (19:12).[23]

It is therefore certain that Christ was put to death by the Romans at the instigation of the Jewish leaders because He bore witness to the truth that He was the Son of God: "In his testimony before Pontius Pilate, [he] made the good confession" (1 Tm. 6:13).

Conclusion

Christ's revelation of His Godhead during His ministry was gradual and mostly indirect, as it had to be, for the Jews were not prepared for a Messiah who would be God incarnate. It was only after the Resurrection that His followers grasped who He was and professed their faith in

Him following in the footsteps of Thomas who had addressed Him as "My Lord and my God" (Jn. 20:28).

It is certain that from the first the faithful addressed Him as "Lord" (Kyrios). The confession of Jesus as Lord is already contained in the ancient prayer "Maranatha" which is Aramaic for "Lord, come" (cf. Apoc. 22:20). In Romans 10:9 and 1 Corinthians 12:3 there is a clear testimony to the confession of Jesus as Lord. In Romans 9:5, a doxology to God is changed into a doxology to Christ.

The Lordship of Christ is understood as extending over the whole of creation, the angelic hosts as well as the visible creation and the world of men, and so the New Testament writers have no hesitation in applying to Him Old Testament texts which referred to Yahweh. Thus St. Paul in Philippians 2:10 applies to Jesus the words found in Isaiah 45:23: "To me every knee shall bow, every tongue shall swear," and the author of Hebrews applies to Him the words of Psalm 102[101]: "Of old you laid the foundation of the earth, and the heavens are the work of your hands" (v. 25).

Strict monotheists though they were, the Apostles and their Jewish converts felt themselves compelled to pay supreme homage to Him whom in His mortal life they had known as Jesus of Nazareth. Worshiping Him as the Lord, the Son of God, they perceived that He was identical with the Jesus of history. The light that during His mortal life was hidden under a bushel had now been put on a lampstand to serve as a light to the nations.

Reflecting on the Master's words and deeds, the disciples perceived that the claims they were making for Him openly after the Resurrection had been made by Him during His public ministry, but less directly and often only by implication, as in His question to the Jewish leaders regarding the interpretation of Psalm 110[109]: "If David thus calls him Lord, how is he his son?" (Mt. 22:45)

The claim that Christ's followers made for Him is unique in the religious history of mankind. As Martin Hengel, commenting on Philippians 2:6-8, well says: "The discrepancy between the shameful death of a Jewish state criminal and the confession that depicts this executed man as a pre-existent divine figure who becomes man and humbles Himself to a slave's death, is, as far as I can see, without analogy in the ancient world." [24]

The disciples of Christ can make this claim because it was first made by Him. Those who had come before Him—Moses and the prophets—are the servants of God; He is the Son who, before Abraham came to be, already was. It was for making this claim that He was crucified. The Liberal Protestant view of Harnack and others, that He was a purely human person, a simple preacher of love toward God and man is now almost everywhere abandoned. The only Christ for whose existence there is any evidence at all is a miracle-worker making stupendous claims.

These claims must be either true or false. That they are true, that Christ was indeed what He said He was—the Son of God, who not only revealed the Father but was one with the Father—is the verdict of Christian faith.

If anyone says the claims are false, he will have to say that Christ, who made them, either knew that they were false or mistakenly thought they were true.

The first alternative is incompatible with the sublimity of His character, to which unbelieving scholars themselves bear witness. Of His holiness Wilhelm Bousset writes: "In His heroic stature and His absolute self-devotion, in His exclusive insistence upon the highest and the best, and His scorning of anything less, He stands perhaps at an unattainable distance from us and ever shows an unbending sternness, nay an awfulness before which we shrink. We cannot presume to measure ourselves against the hero. Yet He remains the conscience of His followers; His words are still the thorn which allows them no rest. With unwavering clearness He points out the way which we must follow, even if He Himself is far beyond our reach." [25]

The second alternative is incompatible with the evident wisdom, the profound sanity, that marks all His discourses, and it may be doubted whether anyone has seriously entertained this view. "No modern critic in his five wits," G. K. Chesterton wrote, "thinks that the preacher of the Sermon on the Mount was a horrible half-witted imbecile that might be scrawling stars upon the walls of a cell.... Upon any possible historical criticism, He must be put higher than that. Yet by all analogy we have really to put Him there or else in the highest place of all."[26]

One may, with Drews and Couchoud, deny that Christ ever existed, or one may hold, with Bultmann, that the Gospels tell us nothing of Christ except that He existed and was crucified. But these are counsels of despair. If one admits that the Gospels provide us with a reliable account of what Christ said and did, then we are faced with a trilemma from which there is no escape: Christ either deceived mankind by conscious fraud, or He was Himself deluded, or He was divine."[27]

Notes

1. *The Interpretation of the New Testament,* 1861-1961, p. 282.

2. *The Christology of the New Testament* (tr. S. Guthrie and Charles A. M. Hall), SCM Press, London & Westminster Press, Philadelphia, 1959, p. 317.

3. *The Teaching of Christ,* Cambridge University Press, 1933, p. 201.

4. Quoted in A. M. Hunter, *The Work and Words of Jesus,* SCM Press, London and Westminster Press, Philadelphia, 1930, p. 79.

5. Cf. C. F. D. Moule, *The Origin of Christology,* Cambridge University Press, 1977, p. 33.

6. *Op. cit.,* p. 8.

7. *New Testament Theology,* p. 266.

8. *The Origin of Christology,* p. 13.

9. *The Gospels and the Jesus of History,* pp. 236-237.

10. *Jesus, Master and Lord,* A. R. Mowbray, London, 1953, p. 205.

11. *The Christology of the New Testament,* p. 56.

12. *Jesus, Master and Lord,* pp. 205-206.

13. *New Testament Theology,* p. 299.

14. *The Gospel According to St. Mark,* MacMillans, London, 1966, p. 121.

15. Cf. *New Testament Theology,* pp. 61-68.

16. *The Parables Then and Now,* SCM Press, London, 1971, pp. 25-26.

17. *New Testament Theology,* p. 251. In Greek, the subject of the verb is usually not expressed by a personal pronoun, this being included in the form of the verb. Hence the "I" in Christ's statement is very emphatic.

18. *According to John,* SCM Press, London, pp. 90-93.

19. *Jesus of Nazareth,* Hodder and Stoughton, London, 1973, p. 163.

20. *Jesus: A Gospel Portrait,* Pflaum Standard, Cincinnati, 1975, p. 155.

21. *Roman Society and Roman Law in the New Testament,* The Clarendon Press, Oxford, 1963, p. 46.

22. *Jesus of Nazareth,* p. 163.

23. Cf. *Sherwin-White, loc. cit.*

24. *The Son of God* (tr. John Bowden), SCM Press, London, 1976, p. 1.

25. Quoted in De Grandmaison, *Jesus Christ,* Sheed & Ward, London, 1935, Vol. II, p. 192.

26. *The Everlasting Man,* Hodder and Stoughton, London, 1925, p. 236.

27. Cf. A. M. Hunter, *The Work and Words of Jesus,* SCM Press, London, 1960, p. 90.

References

L. Bouyer, *The Eternal Son,* Our Sunday Visitor, Huntington, IN, 1978, pp. 168-183. A masterly summary of the evidence bearing on Christ's revelation of Himself.

Oscar Cullmann, *The Christology of the New Testament,* SCM Press, London, 1959. A classical study of the Christological titles in the New Testament. A weakness is Cullmann's conception of revelation as concerned exclusively with the action of God.

Martin Hengel, *The Son of God* (tr. John Bowden), SCM Press, London, 1976. A close-packed study of the term.

Sir Edwin Hoskins and Noel Davey, *The Riddle of the New Testament,* Faber and Faber, London, 1931 (Faber paperback, 1958). Stresses Christological significance of the parables.

A. M. Hunter, *The Work and Words of Jesus,* SCM Press, London, 1950. Pages 80-122 deal with Christ's teaching about Himself.

Joachim Jeremias, *New Testament Theology,* Vol. 1 (tr. John Bowden), SCM Press, London, 1971. Pages 250-299 deal with Jesus' testimony to His mission.

Xavier Léon-Dufour, *The Gospels and the Jesus of History* (tr. John McHugh), Collins, London, 1968. Cf. especially pp. 243-254.

I. Howard Marshall, *The Origins of New Testament Christology,* Inter-Varsity Press, Leicester, 1976. A brief and comparatively conservative survey of the views of modern scholars on the subject.

C. F. D. Moule, *The Origin of Christology,* Cambridge University Press, Cambridge, 1977. Discusses four well-known descriptions of Jesus and lays stress on St. Paul's notion of the corporate Christ.

James T. O'Connor, *The Father's Son,* St. Paul Editions, Boston, 1984. Cf. especially pp. 167-204.

H. E. W. Turner, *Jesus, Master and Lord,* A. R. Mowbray, London, 1953. Pages 185-235 contain a sober appraisal of Christ's teaching about Himself.

VI. The Resurrection of Jesus Christ

The Centrality of the Resurrection in the Gospel

In the New Testament the resurrection of Jesus is no incidental or peripheral matter, but is the major premise of the Christian Faith. On this point scholars of every shade of opinion are agreed. Thus Archbishop Ramsey writes: "For them [the first disciples], the Gospel without the Resurrection was not merely a Gospel without its final chapter; it was not a Gospel at all."[1]

From the first, the Resurrection was the central point of the New Testament message. That Christ who was crucified is risen from the dead was the theme of the sermons of which St. Luke has left us a record in the opening chapters of Acts. Many who heard the message welcomed it and were baptized. The Sanhedrin, upset by these conversions to the new Faith, summoned the Apostles to appear before them and ordered them to desist from preaching this new doctrine. This the Apostles refused to do. "We cannot," they said, "but speak of what we have seen and heard" (Acts 4:20).

For St. Paul, it is the Resurrection of Christ that guarantees the validity of our Christian Faith. "If Christ has not been raised," he writes, "then our preaching is in vain and your faith is in vain.... If Christ has not been raised, your faith is futile and you are still in your sins" (1 Cor. 15:14, 17).

The Apostle is here primarily concerned with what may be called the theological implications of the Resurrection. Through His Death and Resurrection Christ has inaugurated a new era in man's relations with God, and the Christian participates in the blessings of this new era through Baptism. In Baptism, the Christian is associated with Christ in the mystery of Redemption, dying to sin and being made alive to God by the gift of sanctifying grace. This gift is eternal life in germ, its first installment (cf. Heb. 11:1); it associates the believer with Christ in glory (cf. Eph. 2:6), and enables him to meet the demands of this new way of life, to "walk in newness of life" (Rom. 6:4), and set his mind "on things that are above" (Col. 3:2).

St. Peter, too, grounds our Christian hope in the fact of the Resurrection. He writes: "Blessed be the God and Father of our Lord Jesus Christ! By his great mercy we have been born anew to a living hope through the resurrection of Jesus Christ from the dead, and to an inheritance which is imperishable, undefiled, and unfading, kept in heaven for you" (1 Pt. 1:3-4).

It is clear from the Gospels that Jesus viewed His ministry as culminating in His death and resurrection. He is the grain of wheat that must die if it is to bear fruit (cf. Jn. 12:24), the one who must be lifted up in order to draw all men to Himself (cf. Jn. 12:32), He who said of Himself: "I have a baptism to be baptized with; and how I am constrained until it is accomplished" (Lk. 12:50). But, as He foretold on several occasions, His death was to be followed by resurrection (cf. Mk. 8:31; 9:9-13, 31; 10:33-34). These predictions, as the evangelists tell us, fell on deaf ears, for the disciples were expecting a Messiah of a very different kind.

The Resurrection of Jesus, besides having profound theological implications, is of great apologetical significance also. It is the greatest of His miracles and the sign to which He Himself appealed as the guarantee that He came from God. When the Pharisees asked Him for a sign of the authenticity of His mission, He appealed to His coming resurrection: "An evil and adulterous generation seeks for a sign; but no sign shall be given to it except the sign of the prophet Jonah. For as Jonah was three days and three nights in the belly of the whale, so will the Son of Man be three days and three nights in the heart of the earth" (Mt. 12:39-40). His resurrection, to which He referred in cryptic terms, was the miracle that would demonstrate that He had authority to cleanse the Temple (cf. Jn. 2:19), and St. Matthew tells us that the Jewish leaders, knowing of the prophecy, asked Pilate for a guard to prevent its fulfillment (cf. Mt. 27:63-64).

Facts Accepted by All

There are a number of facts that are accepted by all, or nearly all scholars, whether or not they regard the Resurrection of Christ as an event in objective reality involving the return of His dead body to life.

1. At the time of Christ, the Pharisees were looking forward to a resurrection, but this was the eschatological resurrection of all the just at the end of time. The resurrection of an individual did not enter into their concept of the resurrection.

Similarly, the concept of a Messiah who was to die and rise again was quite foreign to their thinking, for they looked forward to the coming of a triumphant Messiah from heaven. They interpreted the passages in Isaiah which refer to a Suffering Servant of God as applying to the people of Israel, not to an individual. Neither the Jewish people in general nor the disciples of Christ were expecting a Messiah who would be put to death and rise again.

2. Christ suffered death by crucifixion as the result of a sentence issued by the Roman procurator, Pontius Pilate, in response to a request from the Jewish authorities, and His body, on being taken from the cross, was buried.

3. The disciples whom Jesus had gathered around Him were thrown into confusion by this turn of events

which upset their most cherished hopes, and thoroughly disheartened, they went into hiding. Peter, their leader, had disowned his Master, and though repentant, was in no state to rally the group.

4. Seven weeks later, at Pentecost, Peter and his associates boldly proclaimed that the Jesus of Nazareth who had been crucified was the long-awaited Messiah. They declared that He had risen from the dead as the Scriptures had foretold and after His resurrection had appeared to them and given them the task of calling others to believe in Him and so obtain forgiveness of their sins.

5. As a result of this preaching, a new movement came into being within the confines of Judaism. Those who believed in Christ were baptized and formed a close-knit community, and even though they continued to worship in the Temple, were from the first distinguished from other Jewish groups, primarily by their faith in the risen Christ.

6. A few years later, a young rabbi named Saul, who had bitterly opposed the new movement, gave it his allegiance as the result of an experience near the city of Damascus. He was on his way there to have the followers of Jesus thrown into prison when he was struck down, and, as he later testified, saw the risen Christ. As a result of this experience he became a follower of Christ and for the next thirty years devoted himself wholeheartedly to the task of bringing others, pagans as well as Jews, to share his faith in Christ.

7. Within a generation, there were communities of Christians, all closely linked by their faith in the risen Christ, in many of the cities and towns of Palestine, Syria, Asia Minor, Macedonia, Greece and Italy. The Catholic Church, to use the term employed later by St. Ignatius of Antioch, had come into being, and had put down roots that would enable it to survive in its struggle with the Roman State which began in 65, with the Neronian persecution.

The Explanation of These Facts

The traditional Christian view of these facts is that they can be accounted for only if we accept the New Testament witness that Christ, whose dead body was placed in the tomb on Good Friday, rose from the dead on Easter Day and, on that day and subsequently, manifested Himself alive in His glorified body to His followers, thereby creating in them the certainty that He had triumphed over death.

In this account of the matter, the risen Christ is the same person, with the same body, as the Jesus of Nazareth who preached and cured the sick in Galilee and Judea, but His humanity has been transformed. "There are," Archbishop Ramsey remarks, "two seemingly contrary features in the narratives of the appearances. On the one hand the narratives describe Jesus acting in a manner reminiscent of the conditions of His life during His earthly ministry. He invites the disciples to touch Him; He breaks bread and eats with them; He walks with them; He assures them in all these ways that He is the same Jesus whom they have known before. On the other hand there are features of the narratives which suggest a mode of life new and utterly unlike the former mode. He is seen only by disciples; He is recognized by them gradually; He appears suddenly and as suddenly disappears. These aspects of the story suggest that if the risen life is indeed bodily, it is bodily with a difference." [2]

This then is the Christian account of the matter—that Jesus who was dead is now alive (cf. Acts 25:19), but is alive not as a disembodied spirit but as a composite of soul and body, because, as St. Peter said when he addressed the Jews on the day of Pentecost, "nor did his flesh see corruption" (Acts 2:31).

If the Resurrection of Christ took place in the manner we have described, it was not only a miraculous event, like the raising of Lazarus from the dead, but was a unique event in the history of mankind. In the course of time those who do not accept the traditional Christian version of the matter have either denied the Resurrection outright or put forward an explanation that is radically different from that put forward by the Church.

We shall deal with these alternative explanations after we have considered the witness of the New Testament texts. However, we note here that most of these explanations are not imposed by a critical study of the New Testament texts, but simply reflect the preconceptions with which the scholars have approached the texts. For one who is committed to the doctrine that miracles are impossible, clearly a genuine resurrection from the dead is out of the question. In such a philosophy there can be no exceptions to the rule that at death the human body enters upon a process of disintegration that is irreversible.

Why the Traditional View Is Unacceptable to the Rationalist

Bultmann expressed this view of the matter with admirable candor when he wrote: "A historical fact which involves a resurrection from the dead is utterly inconceivable."[3] Similarly, Hastings Rashdall rejected the resurrection as incompatible with the laws of nature. "The reanimation, or the sudden transformation into something not quite material and yet not quite spiritual, of a really dead body," he wrote, "would involve the violation of the best ascertained laws of physics, chemistry, and physiology. Were the testimony fifty times stronger than it is, any hypothesis would be more possible than that."[4]

If, on the other hand, one holds that miracles are possible, because God can intervene in His creation to bring about results that are beyond the power of natural causes, then the resurrection of Jesus becomes a question of historical fact, which like any other historical fact is to be answered in the light of the evidence brought forward to show that it really took place.

Although our attention will be concentrated on the evidence for the Resurrection considered as a historical event, it needs to be borne in mind that the resurrection of

Jesus is not an isolated event. It has to be viewed in the context of His claim to be the Son of God, His teaching and His miracles, and of His impact on the course of history through the Church that traces her origin to the Risen Christ. The Resurrection, if it occurred, will certainly have been unique, but so is He for whom the claim is made that He rose from the dead.

The Witness of the New Testament Texts

The Witness of St. Paul

The earliest *written* reference to the resurrection is a brief mention of the fact in St. Paul's First Epistle to the Thessalonians, which most scholars think was written in 50 or 51 (John A. T. Robinson says early 50). There we read that the Thessalonians had "turned to God from idols, to serve a living and true God, and to wait for his Son from heaven, whom he raised from the dead, Jesus who delivers us from the wrath to come" (1:9-10).

But the most significant testimony in St. Paul's Epistles is found in his First Epistle to the Corinthians, which Robinson thinks was written early in 55. There we read, in the 15th chapter:

1. "Now I would remind you, brethren, in what terms I preached to you the gospel, which you received, in which you stand,
2. by which you are saved, if you hold it fast— unless you believed in vain.
3. For I delivered to you as of first importance what I also received, that Christ died for our sins in accordance with the scriptures,
4. that he was buried, that he was raised on the third day in accordance with the scriptures,
5. and that he appeared to Cephas, then to the twelve.
6. Then he appeared to more than five hundred brethren at one time, most of whom are still alive, though some have fallen asleep.

7. Then he appeared to James, then to all the apostles.

8. Last of all, as to one untimely born, he appeared also to me.

9. For I am the least of the apostles unfit to be called an apostle, because I persecuted the Church of God.

10. But by the grace of God I am what I am, and his grace toward me was not in vain. On the contrary, I worked harder than any of them, though it was not I, but the grace of God which is with me.

11. Whether it was I or they, so we preach and so you believed."

It is, in a sense, by chance that we have this clear and striking testimony to the Resurrection, penned about 25 years after the event, for it was occasioned by the fact that some of the faithful in Corinth had been denying the resurrection of the body. What had led them to adopt this view we do not know. They may have been influenced by Platonic philosophy or one of the other systems then in vogue, or they may have imagined that the only resurrection the Christian was to experience was the spiritual resurrection which they had been granted through their faith in Christ.

St. Paul refutes this error by appealing to the Resurrection of Christ, which, in response to his preaching, they had already accepted as a fact. If, the apostle argues, the dead do not rise again—and it is clearly a question of bodily resurrection—then Christ did not rise from the dead. And if Christ did not rise, then their faith is a matter of empty words, and their sins have not been forgiven (cf. vvs. 12-17).

It is agreed by practically all scholars that the passage which begins at verse 3 regarding the death, burial and resurrection of Christ is a stereotyped formula dating from the earliest days of the Church. What St. Paul was *handing on* (a technical term) was what he had *received* (another technical term) as standard Christian teaching. He had received it either at the time of his conversion (i.e., probably about the year 33) or three years later when he went to Jerusalem and spent a fortnight with St. Peter and saw St. James (cf. Acts 9:26-29; Gal. 2:11-14).

There is no agreement, however, among the scholars about where the traditional formula ended. Some think it stopped at the word "appeared" (v. 5); others think it included the reference to Peter and the twelve; others think it went as far as the reference to James and all the apostles (v. 7).

However far the traditional formula extended, what is sure is that St. Paul is citing various witnesses to the fact of the Resurrection of Christ. He gives no details of the appearances, for he is concerned only to establish the fact that He rose from the dead. This Paul does by appealing to the testimony of witnesses, many of whom are still alive and could, if contacted, repeat their testimony. Moreover, it could well be that when he was preaching to the Corinthians a few years earlier, he provided them with some of the detailed information that is recorded in the Gospels.

"Christ died for our sins": from the beginning the death of Christ was regarded as making atonement for our sins, in fulfillment of the Old Testament prophecies, and in particular those to be found in Isaiah 53 (cf. Acts 8:30-35; 1 Pt. 2:21-24).

It is not sure whether it is only the resurrection itself or the fact that it occurred on the third day that is claimed to be a fulfillment of the Old Testament prophecies. It seems more likely that "on the third day" is merely a statement of fact, so that what St. Paul is saying is that Christ rose in fulfillment of the Scriptures (e.g., Ps. 16[15]:10), and did so on the third day. The fact that the Resurrection occurred on the first day of the week accounts for the practice of observing Sunday rather than Saturday as "the Lord's day" in the Apostolic Church (cf. Acts 20:7; 1 Cor. 16:2; Apoc. 1:10).

It has been said that St. Paul in this passage makes no mention of the empty tomb. Thus R. E. Brown writes: "To see a hint of the empty tomb in the reference to Jesus' burial goes beyond the evidence."[5] But this is nonsense.

Since the Apostle has stated that Christ was buried and raised from the dead, he clearly implies that the tomb was empty, and an explicit statement of the fact was quite unnecessary. It would have been self-evident to a Jew that if the body of Christ remained in the tomb, the claim that He had been raised from the dead was false. It is only through a simplistic reading of St. Paul and the witness he gives of the faith of the first disciples in 1 Corinthians 15, Bouyer declares, that we can find in Him and in them belief in a resurrection without an empty tomb. "The fragment of primitive kerygma which is preserved for us in verses 3 to 5," Bouyer adds, "opposes Christ's Resurrection not only to His death but also to His burial. Either this is without meaning, or we must conclude that what did rise, in the experience of the first Christians, was the very body that had been put in the tomb."[6] With this verdict G. O. Collins concurs: "For St. Paul to assert that God has raised Jesus from the dead necessarily implies a passage from the tomb."[7]

It will be noticed that St. Paul's list of witnesses differs from that which can be derived from the Gospel narratives. For example, he makes no mention of the appearance to the holy women, perhaps because of the Jewish notion that the testimony of women was unreliable. On the other hand, there is no mention in the Gospels of an appearance to James, and it is unlikely that the appearance to the five hundred to which St. Paul refers is to be identified with the appearance in Galilee of which St. Matthew writes (28:16).

St. Paul puts the appearance of the risen Lord on the road to Damascus which caused his conversion in the same class as the earlier appearances to the Apostles and disciples. Clearly, he was convinced that he had come face to face with Jesus, now risen from the dead and exalted, and that this experience, like the earlier ones, was objective. Elsewhere (2 Cor. 12:1) he speaks of "visions and revelations" which he had received, but it is certain that he did not regard these ecstatic visions as of the same kind as that on the Damascus road, which was, he says, the last of the appearances of the risen Lord to His disciples (1 Cor. 15:8).

After establishing from the fact of Christ's resurrection that we Christians are to rise from the dead, the Apostle goes on to say that Christ's resurrection is the model of that which awaits us; He is "the first fruits of those who have fallen asleep" (v. 20). Then, to lessen the difficulty of understanding how the resurrection of our bodies will be brought about, he appeals to some of the transformations that take place in the natural world, such as that whereby the grain of wheat becomes a plant (v. 37). The bodies we now possess will, he says, be transformed into "spiritual bodies," similar to the glorified body of Christ (v. 44). That is, they will be transformed by the Spirit of God and adapted for existence in the new redeemed order of the Age to Come. This transformation, he tells us, will be effected at the Second Coming of Christ in those who are still alive at the time without their having to undergo decomposition in the grave (v. 51).

From this it follows that there is no force in the argument of G. W. H. Lampe that since Christ was like us in all things but sin (Heb. 4:15), "His body must have decomposed in the grave as ours do."[8] The New Testament witness is quite clear—the body of Christ did *not* decompose in the grave—and the weight of this testimony is not lessened in the least by an argument based on a single verse of Hebrews wrenched from its context.

"We can best sum up the evidence of St. Paul," H. E. W. Turner writes, "as follows: He puts us accidentally in possession of the information that at a stage prior to the compilation of the Canonical Gospels the Church was familiar with an ordered and relatively full narrative of the bare facts. So far from the Gospel tradition being an embroidery on an earlier and simpler tradition, it represents a mere selection of the material available for the purpose."[9]

The Witness of the Gospels

The Gospels, in the form in which we now have them, are almost certainly the product of literary activity extending over several years, and they reached their present form several decades after the events they report. They record an oral tradition that was developed in the Church as her preachers and teachers sought to communicate the Gospel message to Jewish and Gentile believers.

This oral tradition, it must be remembered, was formulated under the scrutiny of those who had witnessed the ministry of Christ and His passion and death, and these witnesses included not only His followers but also His adversaries. As Vincent Taylor has remarked, neither the disciples of Christ nor the Jewish leaders disappeared from the scene in 30 A.D.

The evangelists selected their material from this oral tradition, and to some extent shaped it in accordance with their theological purposes, stressing the features that were in harmony with the portrait of Christ and His mission which they were concerned to paint, in order to strengthen the faith of their readers. It has been remarked, for example, that St. Luke keeps Jerusalem at the center of his story. "His theme is the going up of Jesus to Jerusalem to die, the redemption wrought in Jerusalem, the continuity of the divine purpose through the events in Jerusalem, the mission of the Church from Jerusalem, the advance of the Gospel from Jerusalem to Rome." [10]

The evangelists were not much concerned with things about which a modern historian would have been careful, such as the time and place of events or their sequence. So we find discrepancies in their accounts of the same event. But these are not such as to create doubt about the substance of the event itself. As G. E. Ladd remarks, "We may expect to find variation in important details, but a sound memory as to major events," and he illustrates with his own experience of an event of which he had a vivid memory, but put on the wrong day of the week. [11]

The Gospel Accounts of the Resurrection

The Gospels are unanimous in asserting that the tomb in which Christ had been buried was found empty on Easter Day and that Christ appeared alive to His followers after this discovery. But this substantial unanimity is accompanied by discrepancies in the details of the Gospel accounts. The significance of these discrepancies has been much exaggerated, as if they entitled us to doubt the truth of the main story. But if the Gospels embody independent traditions, as is almost certainly the case, such discrepancies are to be expected.

"It is a common experience for a lawyer," Norman Anderson writes, "to note how a number of witnesses will almost invariably give accounts which differ widely from each other, initially at least, about any incident at which they have all been present. Each individual will see it from a different angle (both literally and metaphorically), will note some but by no means all of the relevant facts, and will usually be highly selective in what he actually remembers. To a considerable degree, therefore, minor differences in some of the Resurrection stories may be regarded as actually strengthening the evidence rather than weakening it; for if a number of witnesses tell exactly the same story, with no divergence, it is nearly always a sign that they have been 'coached' as to what they should say, or at least have conferred together on the subject." Moreover, he adds, it is very probable that some of the discrepancies would be removed and some of the omissions explained if we were able to cross-examine the witnesses, something that is now impossible.[12]

A. Divergences in the Record

There is a divergence in the accounts of the women who went to visit the tomb on Easter morning. All three Synoptics mention Mary Magdalen and Mary, the mother of James; St. Mark adds the name of Salome and St. Luke that of Joanna. St. John mentions only Mary Magdalen, but he tells us that when she reported her experience to Peter and John, she said: "They have taken the body and *we* do not know where they have laid him," which implies that there were others with her.

St. Mark and St. Luke tell us that the women came to anoint the body of Jesus, whereas St. John tells us that Nicodemus bound the body with myrrh and aloes before laying it in the tomb (19:39-40). The Synoptics tell us that the body of Jesus was wrapped in a shroud (sindon), whereas St. John seems to say that it was wrapped in strips of linen cloth (othonia). It seems, however, that the word St. John uses *could* refer to a shroud.

More serious, in the opinion of some scholars, is the divergence in the Gospel accounts of where the post-resurrection appearances took place. St. Matthew speaks of an appearance to the women in Jerusalem, reports the message of an angel that Jesus wanted the disciples to meet Him in Galilee, and speaks of a final meeting in Galilee.

In the opening verses of his 16th chapter St. Mark reports the same message but has no record of any appearance of Jesus in Jerusalem. St. Luke, as we have said, mentions only appearances in Jerusalem—to the two disciples on the way to Emmaus and to the Eleven.

St. John relates the appearance to Mary Magdalen and two appearances, a week apart, to the disciples in Jerusalem, and in the final chapter of his Gospel records an appearance in Galilee.

A number of contemporary scholars, following Kirsopp Lake, think there could not have been appearances in both Jerusalem and Galilee, and opt for Galilee.

Lake, who put forward this theory in 1907, held that after the Crucifixion the Apostles returned at once to Galilee. There they heard of the discovery of the empty tomb, had some kind of visionary experience which restored their faith in Christ, and returned to Jerusalem, where they met the women who told them of their discovery of the empty tomb, which they mistakenly believed to be the tomb in which Christ had been buried.[13]

This theory that the appearances, which were of course only subjective, took place only in Galilee was adopted by Rudolf Bultmann and has been favorably received by some Neo-Modernist scholars.

Thus Fr. G. O'Collins writes: "It seems most plausible to hold that the disciples' encounters with Jesus took place in Galilee. They learned of the empty tomb only after their return to Jerusalem. They had in any case played no role either in Jesus' death or burial or in the discovery of the empty tomb." [14]

He admits that "it is possible to reconcile the stories and have the disciples speeding back and forth between Jerusalem and Galilee." [15] O'Collins greatly exaggerates the difficulty, for the distance is not great—about eighty miles—and there was ample time—forty days—for the journey to Galilee and back to Jerusalem. The disciples could therefore have traveled at a leisurely pace; no speeding was required. Moreover, this theory would imply that St. Luke's account of the meeting on the way to Emmaus is no more than pious fiction, and the same would have to be said of St. John's account of the visit of Peter and John to the empty tomb and the accounts in St. Luke and John of the appearances to the apostolic group in Jerusalem.

Similarly, Fr. R. E. Brown declares that "we must reject the thesis that the Gospels can be harmonized through a rearrangement whereby Jesus appeared several times to the Twelve, first in Jerusalem and then in Galilee." [16]

The fact is that on this matter of where the appearances occurred the Gospels can be harmonized without much difficulty. "The best solution of the difficulty," H. E. W. Turner writes, "appears to be also the simplest; namely, that the two traditions supplement each other. A short stay in Jerusalem, for perhaps a week after the Resurrection, was followed by a return to Galilee and a final return to Jerusalem in time for the Feast of Pentecost. The forty-day period mentioned in the Acts could cover just such a time-table. It is perhaps slightly surprising that the only Evangelist who raises any difficulties on this hypothesis (Luke) is precisely the one who records the chronological datum necessary for its acceptance." [17]

B. Harmonization Is Possible

No one will pretend that it is possible to remove all the difficulties created by the discrepancies in the various Gospel accounts, but it is, as Anderson remarks, a matter of plain common sense to make a reasonable attempt to resolve apparent inconsistencies in any web of evidence before jumping to the premature conclusion that the witnesses—or, indeed, one and the same witness—have presented us with "glaring" and "irreconcilable" contradictions.[18] And the fact is that the Gospel accounts can be in great measure harmonized. M. J. Lagrange, the great biblical scholar, writes: "The four evangelists relate, each in his own way, how the tomb of Jesus was found empty, to the great astonishment of Christ's friends.... The difficulty of harmonizing the four accounts has been greatly exaggerated. Nothing is more simple, provided we do not stick at unimportant details, provided also we pay attention to the way in which each Gospel was composed."[19]

Dorothy Sayers is a playwright who had to immerse herself in the New Testament documents, and she remarks how apparent contradictions often turn out to be not truly contradictory but supplementary. "Take for example," she writes, "the various accounts of the Resurrection appearances at the Sepulcher. The divergences appear very great at first sight; and much ink and acrimony have been expended in proving that certain of the stories are not 'original' or 'authentic,' but are accretions grafted upon the first-hand reports by the pious imagination of Christians. Well, it may be so. But the fact remains that *all* of them without exception, can be made to fall into place in a single, orderly, coherent narrative without the smallest contradiction or difficulty, and without any suppression, invention or manipulation beyond a trifling effort to *imagine* the natural behavior of a group of startled people running about in the dawn light between Jerusalem and the Garden."[20]

C. Harmonization of the Narratives of the Resurrection

The state of the evidence is such that a wholly satisfactory harmonization of the various narratives is not possible. But notwithstanding the difficulty of reconciling the different accounts, such a harmonization is not without its value as showing that the divergences are not so wide as is sometimes stated.

G. E. Ladd has proposed the following tentative harmonization:

1. The earthquake and the removal of the stone before dawn on Sunday.
2. A group of four women come early to the tomb, wondering who will move the stone. As they approach they are amazed to see that the stone has been rolled away.
3. Mary rushes off to tell Peter and John that the body has been stolen (Jn. 20:2).
4. The other women stay in the garden. They enter the tomb and are met by two angels who tell them to carry word of the Resurrection to the disciples. Matthew speaks of an angel (28:5), Mark of a young man (16:5), Luke of two men (24:4) and a vision of angels (24:23). This is one more example of the divergences in the Synoptics regarding matters of detail.
5. The women rush away from the garden, filled with mingled emotions of fear and joy, speaking to no one about the vision of angels at the empty tomb (Mk. 16:8).
6. Later in the day, Jesus met the women. (Matthew does *not* say that this meeting occurred in the garden.) They had run away from the tomb. Jesus tells them to bear the word to the disciples; they depart to find the disciples who are not together but scattered (Mt. 26:56).
7. Peter and John, having been informed by Mary, come to the tomb after the women have left.

They see the burial cloths; vague comprehension dawns on John. They rush off together to gather the disciples.

8. Mary returns to the tomb after Peter and John have left; they had run to the tomb (Jn. 20:4), leaving Mary behind. She still thinks the body has been stolen. She is weeping outside, knowing nothing of the experience of the women she has left in the garden. She sees the two angels, then Jesus (Jn. 20:11-17).

9. After the first shock of amazement has worn off, the women find some of the disciples; the disciples cannot believe the fanciful story (Lk. 24:11).

10. The disciples are gathered together.

11. Mary arrives and tells of her experience (Jn. 20:18).

12. That afternoon the two disciples meet Jesus on the way to Emmaus.

13. Some time that afternoon Jesus appears to Peter (Lk. 24:34).

14. That evening, the disciples are gathered in a closed room. They had been scattered, but the testimony of the women, of Peter and John, and then of Mary, serves to bring them all together. Thomas is absent.

15. A second appearance to the Eleven, including Thomas, a week later.

16. An appearance in Galilee (Mt. 28:16). The appearance by the lake of Tiberias (Jn. 21) and to five hundred brethren (1 Cor. 15:6).

17. Return of the disciples to Jerusalem; final appearance and ascension.[21]

This is only a tentative harmonization and it may not correspond with the order of the facts, for our sources do not provide us with enough information to check the details. But these sources are unanimous in testifying to the central facts—that the tomb was found empty, and this was not because the body had been stolen but because

Christ had risen from the dead—a fact of which the disciples became convinced through seeing Him alive.

The force of this testimony is strengthened by some vivid passages which put us in touch with what looks very much like first-hand evidence. Such are the story of the walk to Emmaus by Cleopas and his unnamed companion, the recognition of Jesus by Mary when He called her by name, and the perception by Peter and John that the burial cloths had been disturbed.

The evangelists do not describe the Resurrection itself, because no one witnessed it. Indeed, it is hard to see how it could have been described by any witness had one been there, since it involved the complete transformation of the humanity of Christ. Similarly, it is very doubtful whether the Resurrection was the kind of event that could have been registered by a motion picture camera had one been there.

It is clear from the Gospels that the risen Christ and the Jesus who was crucified are the same identical person. This is clearly implied in the words: "See my hands and my feet, that it is I myself; handle me, and see; for a spirit has not flesh and bones as you see that I have" (Lk. 24:39). The Resurrection therefore involved the resuscitation of the corpse that was laid in the tomb. But it was no mere resuscitation such as Lazarus experienced, for the body of the risen Christ possessed new properties. He could appear and vanish at will, allow Himself to be recognized or hide His identity. There was therefore transformation as well as continuity. The body of Christ is a real body, the same body as He had in His mortal life, but it is what St. Paul called a "spiritual body"—a body that has been transformed and possesses some of the properties of spiritual beings.

Alternative Explanations

It is nearly two thousand years since the date of the Resurrection, and during that time various alternative explanations have been put forward by those who have refused to accept the traditional Christian view that Christ really rose from the dead. Many of these theories have been discarded, but from time to time one or another of them is revived. They are therefore worth discussing, for their ineffectiveness throws the strength of the traditional view into bolder relief.

1. The Jewish leaders maintained that the whole business was a case of fraud: the disciples stole the body and then proclaimed that their Master had risen from the dead.

That the tomb was empty on Easter morning was a fact on which all were agreed.

The Jewish leaders, rejecting the Resurrection as the explanation of this fact, offered the only other plausible explanation available to them, namely, that the body had been stolen.

This theory of conscious deception on the part of the Apostles accounts for the vehemence with which Saul persecuted the first Christians—he thought they were blasphemous liars.

However, it has few supporters nowadays, for it goes against all the evidence.

It is clear that the Apostles were dispirited by the death of Christ, were not expecting a resurrection, and were in no mood to antagonize the Sanhedrin by removing the body. Moreover, such a fraud is quite out of harmony with their character as it is revealed to us in the Gospels. Nor would they have anything to gain by such a fraud, either in this world, where they were to be persecuted for proclaiming the Resurrection, or in the next, where they could expect a severe judgment for bearing false witness.

This explanation was put forward once again in the 18th century by Reimarus, who added that the Apostles waited fifty days before announcing the Resurrection, by which time the body would have been unrecognizable. Origen in the 3rd century had already disposed of this suggestion by pointing out that men do not risk their lives and suffer martyrdom for a lie (cf. Acts 12:2).

2. Another theory is that Christ did not really die, but was laid unconscious in the tomb. Recovering from His

wounds, He appeared to His disciples. They, thinking He had been dead, concluded that He had risen from the dead. Paulus, a German scholar, put this view forward early in the 19th century, and in our own time Hugh Schonfeld has put forward a similar theory in his book *The Passover Plot.*

This theory supposes that those who were on the spot and were sure they had seen Christ die were mistaken. And is it likely that His enemies would have failed to make sure He was really dead? Even if Christ did not die, how could the appearance of a half-dead man account for the transformation that took place in the disciples?

3. Another theory is that the body was thrown into a common grave, from which it did not emerge.

This would have been contrary to the Roman practice, which was to put the body at the disposal of the relatives. And the Gospels tell us that Pilate did this at the request of Joseph of Arimathea. A variant of this theory proposed early in this century by Kirsopp Lake held that the women went to the wrong tomb, which they found empty, and were directed to another where the body lay. They were frightened at the detection of their errand and fled, understanding only imperfectly or not at all what they had heard. Later on, they came to believe that the young man who had spoken to them was announcing the Resurrection, that the empty tomb was the one in which Jesus had been buried.

Had there been any mistake about the tomb, it would have been speedily corrected by the Sanhedrin when the Apostles began to proclaim the Resurrection. But, as we have said, the Sanhedrin knew as well as anyone that the tomb in which Christ had been buried was empty.

4. Ernest Renan suggested that the holy women were moved by their love of Jesus to imagine that He had risen and departed for Galilee, and their assurance was so strong that it created a similar conviction in the minds of the Apostles.

This theory breaks down on the fact that the Apostles were hard-headed men, not the sort to be swayed by women's fancies. Indeed, the Gospels report that their first reaction to the message of the women was to dismiss it as the product of their imagination.

5. Some have urged that the Apostles were led to believe in the Resurrection by visions they experienced. These were either subjective (J. Weiss, Bultmann) or objective (Pannenberg), but they did not involve a sensory experience of the physical body of Christ, that had been laid in the tomb.

When we come to inquire what was the objective reality to which these visions bore witness, we get a variety of answers. For Willi Marxsen, it is the continuing influence of Christ in the world of men, the continued existence of the cause for which He died. For others, it is the survival of His immortal soul, which has the power of communicating spiritual life to those who have faith in Him. For others, it is a newly-created spiritual body, distinct from His mortal one, which remained in the tomb. This last theory has been put forward tentatively by a number of authors, who, because they hold there cannot be a disembodied spirit, reject the common teaching that in the Resurrection the soul of Jesus was reunited to His body after being separated from it for about thirty-six hours. As Bouyer has pointed out, there is nothing essentially new in any of these theories, which simply reflect the philosophical prejudices of their authors, and all in one form or another have been refuted long ago.[22]

They cannot be reconciled with the Gospel testimony that the Apostles who were not prepared for the Resurrection saw Christ in many different circumstances and had no doubts about the objective reality of what they saw with their bodily eyes. To their testimony we may add that of the five hundred (1 Cor. 15:6); there is no plausibility in the hypothesis that this was a case of mass illusion.

6. It has been said (e.g., by Lloyd Geering) that the Resurrection story is due to the infiltration of pagan myths of dying and rising gods into the original message of the Gospel.

The fatal objection to this theory is that from the first the Resurrection of Christ was proclaimed as a historical event which occurred in Palestine during the reign of the emperor Tiberius (probably in 30 A.D.), whereas the myths are pictorial representations of timeless truths about natural phenomena, such as the coming of spring and the renewal of plant life. Moreover, any such infiltration would have been prevented by the abhorrence the Christians felt for the pagan cults, described by St. Paul as a form of devil-worship (1 Cor. 10:20).

Conclusion

These and similar explanations are desperate hypotheses developed by those who are unwilling to accept the Gospel story of the empty tomb and the appearances of the risen Christ as a statement of historical fact. The central fact, however inexplicable it may be in terms of the causes with which the secular historian is familiar, is so well attested to that it is unreasonable not to accept it as something that occurred in Palestine early in the fourth decade of our era.

Indeed, B. F. Westcott contends that no historical event of that time is better attested to than the Resurrection of Christ. He writes: "Taking all the evidence together, it is not too much to say that there is no single historic incident better or more variously supported than the Resurrection of Christ. Nothing but the antecedent assumption that it must be false could have suggested the idea of deficiency in the proof of it.... In any ordinary matter of life the evidence would be amply sufficient to determine our action and belief." [23]

Notes

1. *The Resurrection of Christ,* Collins (Fontana), London, 1961, p. 9.

2. *The Resurrection of Christ,* pp. 46-47.

3. Quoted in G. E. Ladd, *I Believe in the Resurrection of Jesus,* Hodder & Stoughton, London, 1975, p. 11.

4. Quoted in De Grandmaison, *Jesus Christ,* Vol. III, p. 157.

5. The Virginal Conception and Bodily Resurrection of Jesus, Geoffrey Chapman, London, 1974, pp. 83-84.

6. *The Eternal Son,* Our Sunday Visitor, Huntington, 1978, p. 204.

7. *The Easter Jesus,* Darton, Longman & Todd, London, 1973, p. 44.

8. *The Resurrection: A Dialogue,* G. W. H. Lampe and D. M. McKinnon, A. R. Mowbray, London, 1966, p. 97.

9. *Jesus, Master and Lord,* A. R. Mowbray, London, 1853, p. 351.

10. *The Resurrection of Christ,* Ramsey, pp. 66-67.

11. *I Believe in the Resurrection of Jesus,* p. 77.

12. *A Lawyer Among the Theologians,* Hodder & Stoughton, London, 1973, pp. 109-110.

13. *The Historical Evidence for the Resurrection of Jesus Christ,* Williams & Norgate, London, 1907.

14. *The Easter Jesus,* Darton, Longman & Todd, London, 1973, p. 29.

15. *Ibid.,* p. 22.

16. *The Virginal Conception and Bodily Resurrection of Jesus,* p. 106.

17. *Jesus, Master and Lord,* H. E. W. Turner, p. 366.

18. *A Lawyer Among the Theologians,* p. 111.

19. *The Gospel of Christ,* Burns, Oates & Washbourne, London, 1938, Vol. II, p. 283.

20. *The Man Born To Be King,* Victor Gollancz, London, 1943, p. 35.

21. Cf. *Believe in the Resurrection of Jesus,* G. E. Ladd, pp. 91-93.

22. Cf. *The Eternal Son,* pp. 201-205. Cf. *Resurrection and the Message of Easter,* León-Dufour, Collins, London, 1974, pp. 239, 320.

23. *The Gospel of the Resurrection,* MacMillan, London, 4th ed., 1889, p. 115.

References

Norman Anderson, *A Lawyer Among the Theologians,* Hodder & Stoughton, London, 1973. As a legal expert, Anderson evaluates the evidence for the Resurrection, pp. 66-149.

Pierre Benoit, O.P., *The Passion and Ressurection of Christ,* (tr. B. Weatherhead), Darton, Longman & Todd, London, 1969.

R. E. Brown, *The Virginal Conception and Bodily Resurrection of Jesus,* G. Chapman, London, 1974. Exaggerates the difficulty of harmonizing the Gospel accounts.

C. F. Evans, *The Resurrection and the New Testament,* SCM Press, London, 1970.

R. H. Fuller, *The Formation of the Resurrection Narratives,* SPCK, London, 1972. This contains a good deal of very speculative theorizing.

G. E. Ladd, *I Believe in the Resurrection of Jesus,* Hodder & Stoughton, London, 1975. A consideration of the evidence by a conservative Protestant scholar.

G. W. H. Lampe and D. M. MacKinnon, *The Resurrection,* A. R. Mowbray, London, 1966. A dialogue between Lampe, a liberal, and MacKinnon, a conservative.

X. León-Dufour, *Resurrection and the Message of Easter,* Collins, London, 1974. Spoiled by the author's commitment to an Existentialist philosophy, which colors his interpretation of the evidence.

Willi Marxsen, *The Resurrection of Jesus of Nazareth* (tr. M. Kohl), SCM Press, London, 1970. For Marxsen, Christ survives only in the survival of His cause.

F. Morison, *Who Moved the Stone?* Faber & Faber, London, 1930. A close study of the Gospel texts, and still in print after 50 years.

G. O'Collins, S.J., *The Easter Jesus,* Darton, Longman & Todd, London, 1973.

M. Ramsey, *The Resurrection of Christ,* Collins (Fontana), London, 1961. A valuable study by the former Archbishop of Canterbury.

H. E. W. Turner, *Jesus, Master and Lord,* A. R. Mowbray, London, 1953, pp. 345-373. A judicious study by an Anglican scholar.

VII. The Church

Among the many millions who profess their faith in the risen Christ and acknowledge Him as their Lord, there is one body that claims Him as the Founder from whom she, and she alone, has received the fullness of divine revelation, and with it, the power to expound this revelation with authority. This is the Catholic Church. She is not an amalgam of the various bodies that bear the Christian name, nor "that segment of humanity which hopes for the future of the world because of its fundamental faith in Christ."[1]

This visible society, the Mystical Body of Christ, is, in the words of the Second Vatican Council, "the sole Church of Christ which in the creed we profess to be one, holy, catholic and apostolic, which our Savior, after His resurrection, entrusted to Peter's pastoral care (cf. Jn. 21:17), commissioning him and the other Apostles to extend and rule it (cf. Mt. 28:18ff.), and which He raised up for all ages as 'the pillar and the mainstay of the truth' (1 Tm. 3:15). This Church, constituted and organized as a society in the present world, subsists in the Catholic Church, which is governed by the successor of Peter and the bishops who are in communion with Him."[2]

In this passage, as the Declaration in Defense of the Catholic Doctrine on the Church (July 5, 1973), made clear, the term "subsists" signifies "identical with." Just as human nature subsists or exists only in individual human beings, so the Church which was founded by Christ exists only in the Church that is governed by the successor of

Peter and the bishops that are in communion with Him.

The description provided by the Council therefore does not differ essentially from the definition formulated by St. Robert Bellarmine: "The visible society of the validly baptized faithful, united in one organized body by the profession of the same Christian Faith, by participation in the same sacraments, and by submission to their legitimate pastors, and in particular to the one Vicar of Christ on earth, the Roman Pontiff." [3]

The term "the Catholic Church" was used by Saint Ignatius of Antioch to designate the Church that is spread over the whole world.[4] Half a century later, the term was used to differentiate the Church of which St. Polycarp was the head from the various heretical and schismatic sects in the city of Smyrna.[5] This Church, which has from the second century called herself "the Catholic Church" maintains that she is identical with the Church of the New Testament, as the mustard tree is identical with the seed from which it sprang. She maintains also that her coming into being and her continuance in being through the centuries is not an accident of history, but was foreseen and willed by Christ during His earthly life as the visible embodiment of the Kingdom of God.

The Kingdom of God

When Christ began His ministry, the Jewish people were looking forward to the coming of a great king who would inaugurate a theocratic kingdom that would take in the whole world and last forever. Tacitus in his *Histories* speaks of this hope entertained by the Jews, a hope based on ancient writings that were in the keeping of the Jewish priests, and fulfilled, in the opinion of Tacitus, in the persons of Vespasian and Titus, who came from the East to assume the government of the world.[6]

The Jewish expectation of the promised Messiah was quickened during the reign of Herod the Great, the first non-Jew to occupy the throne in Jerusalem. People were beginning to wonder if the time was approaching when the prophecy of Jacob was to be fulfilled: "The scepter shall not depart from Judah, nor the ruler's staff from between his feet, until he comes to whom it belongs; and to him shall be the obedience of the peoples" (Gn. 49:10).

Christ began His ministry by calling the whole nation to repent and to accept His teaching so as to be ready to enter the kingdom of God which He had come to inaugurate. In the Sermon on the Mount He set out the dispositions required for entry into the kingdom, and in His parables He outlined its growth and development and its final consummation.

At first, His hearers responded with enthusiasm, but this enthusiasm, based as it was on a misapprehension about the nature of the kingdom, faded, and after the feeding of the five thousand He was led to concentrate His attention on the "little flock" of His disciples, and in particular the group of Twelve whom He chose that they might be constantly with Him (Mk. 3:14).

The New Covenant

In choosing the Twelve, whom He instructed in the secrets of the kingdom, Jesus was preparing to establish a new covenant which would displace the covenant sealed in blood on Sinai, and so would bring into being a new people of God.

He was paving the way for the fulfillment of the prophecy of Jeremiah: "Behold, the days are coming, says the Lord, when I will make a new covenant with the house of Israel and the house of Judah, not like the covenant which I made with their fathers when I took them by the hand to bring them out of the land of Egypt, my covenant which they broke, though I was their husband, says the Lord. But this is the covenant which I will make with the house of Israel after those days, says the Lord: I will put my law within them, and I will write it upon their hearts; and I will be their God, and they shall be my people. And no longer shall each man teach his neighbor and each his brother, saying, 'Know the Lord,' for they shall all know me, from the least of them to the greatest, says the Lord; for I will forgive their iniquity, and I will remember their sin no more" (31:31-34).

It is probable that what Jeremiah directly had in mind was a spiritual renewal that would take place when the people of Israel returned from exile in Babylon. Whether his prophetic vision embraced a distant future we cannot say. What is certain is that the New Testament writers understood the prophecy as predicting the establishment of the new order of things that has come into being through the death and resurrection of Christ.

God, they declare, has established a new covenant and created for Himself a new people, the "Israel of God" (Gal. 6:16). This new Israel is not a single nation, but embraces people "from every nation, from all tribes and peoples and tongues" (Apoc. 7:9). Christ's prophecy has been fulfilled that many would come from the East and the West and sit down at the Messianic banquet with Abraham and Isaac and Jacob (Mt. 8:11).

At the Last Supper Christ declared that He was establishing a new covenant in His blood (Mk. 14:24; Lk. 22:20; 1 Cor. 11:25). This theme, which Christ so succinctly stated, is developed at greater length in the New Testament documents.

In chapter 4 of his Epistle to the Galatians, St. Paul speaks of the two covenants, one the old covenant established on Mt. Sinai and represented by Hagar, a slave and the mother of slave children, the other the new covenant represented by Sarah, a free woman and the mother of free people, who are heirs of the promise made to Abraham.

In chapter 3 of the First Corinthians St. Paul speaks of himself as a minister of the new covenant. This covenant is not inscribed on tables of stone, as the old covenant was, but in the hearts of men. It is spiritual, filled with divine glory, and those who commit themselves to living under this covenant are assured of justification and righteousness, leading to heavenly glory.

The author of the Epistle to the Hebrews argues at length that the Old Covenant has given way to the New, and he quotes Jeremiah 31 as warrant for this claim that the Old Law, and with it the Levitical priesthood, have become obsolete with the coming of Christ.

The Beginnings of the Church

With the establishment of the new covenant, a new people of God has come into being. This is the Church— "the church of the Lord which he obtained with his own blood" (Acts 20:28).

This Church, the new Israel, was from the first an organized community, like the old Israel, which in the designs of God it was to displace.

The Acts of the Apostles is St. Luke's account of the origin and growth of this new institution, from its beginnings in Jerusalem at Pentecost in the year 30 to the arrival of St. Paul in the year 60 as a prisoner in Rome, to be welcomed there by a flourishing Christian community.

In his sermon on the day of Pentecost, St. Peter declared that the prophecy of Joel (2:28-32) has been fulfilled with the outpouring of the Holy Spirit on the disciples of Christ. Through the death and resurrection of Christ a new era has begun in the relations between God and His people, and all men are now invited to become disciples of Christ through faith and Baptism. On that day, we are told, three thousand proclaimed their faith in Christ and were baptized.

Through their reception of Baptism the believers became members of a community, which, although it made its way at first within the confines of Judaism, was seen to be a separate group, distinct from the main body of Judaism. They were "the church" (Acts 5:11; 8:1, 3; 9:31), a body composed of "hearers of the word" (2:41), "the saved" (2:47), "the believers" (5:14). Later, at Antioch, they were to be called "Christians" (11:26). The Jews who remained aloof from the new movement recognized their separateness, calling them a "heresy" (24:5; 28:22).

The members of the new group continued to frequent the Temple and observe the Mosaic ordinances regarding circumcision and the kinds of food it was lawful to eat (cf. Acts 10:14). But already they had their own observances, in particular the Eucharistic meal (2:42), and their own governing body, "the Twelve," of which St. Peter was the head.

Although the Gospel message was at first addressed to Jews and proselytes (pagans who were thinking of adopting Judaism), it was not long before non-Jews with no associations with Judaism were being invited to believe in Christ. There was a mission to Samaria, where the converts were confirmed by Peter and John (8:14-17). Philip the deacon baptized the eunuch of the Queen of the Ethiopians and himself an Ethiopian (8:26-39), and Peter, enlightened by a heavenly vision, baptized the centurion Cornelius (10:1-48).

The flow of converts from paganism increased dramatically after the Apostles were dispersed by the persecution of Herod Agrippa I in 43, and the question of the relationship between the Mosaic Law and the Gospel became acute. It was settled at a Council of Jerusalem in which the Apostles and the elders took part (Acts 15). The decree of the Council freed the non-Jews from the yoke of the Law of Moses, but imposed a few restrictions, so that where Jews and non-Jews lived together, the Jews would not be offended by such things as the eating of blood or of animals that had been strangled.

From this it is clear that the Church from the beginning knew herself to be a corporate entity, distinct from the Synagogue. And this view of her was shared by the Jewish leaders and rulers like Herod Agrippa I. For the Apostles and their disciples, the new religion was the full and perfect form of divinely revealed religion, of which Judaism was but the preparatory phase. Men were now to be linked to one another, not by ties of blood, but by their common calling to faith in Christ.

It seems that for some time the Apostles and their followers entertained the hope that the whole Jewish people would come to faith in Christ, and it may well be that this hope led them to continue to worship in the Temple

and observe the customs of their people (cf. Acts 16:3;
18:18; 20:16; 21:23-26). This hope, as we know, was dis-
appointed, for the bulk of the Jewish people refused to
accept the Gospel.

Summing up, it is clear from the Acts of the Apostles
and the Epistles of St. Paul that from the first those who
believed in Christ formed a distinct social group, a visible
society, which had clearly-defined limits and was governed
by a hierarchy which based its claim to teach with authority and to rule, not on any elective process but on direct
appointment by Christ.

The Church Was Established by Christ as a Visible Society

The Church Was Established by Christ

It is clear from the Acts of the Apostles that the
Church was not brought into existence by a movement of
enthusiasm among believers in Christ, nor by the intelligence of the Apostles, but owes her existence to the action
of Christ, who laid the foundations by His preaching and
built on these when He sent His Spirit as He had promised
to do before His passion.

The Rationalist hypotheses regarding the origin of the
Church are of two main kinds:
   a) the Church came into being spontaneously as the
      result of an instinctive movement created by the
      preaching and example of Christ;
   b) the Church was created by the Apostles when their
      hopes of the Second Coming of Christ (the *Pa-
      rousia)* began to fade.

The first of these hypotheses is incompatible with the
fact that from the first the Church had a definite organization. Vague religious impulses take time to give rise to
concrete institutions, and in this case the time was not
available.

The second hypothesis cannot be reconciled with the
fact made plain by the documents that what brought the

Church into being was the resurrection of Christ. Those who deny the fact of the Resurrection naturally have to look for some other explanation of the origin of the Church.

The Apostles constantly declare that the Church was founded by Christ and that they are His servants. He is the foundation on which they are building, the head of the Body, of which they and the rest of the faithful are members; the good tidings which they bring is His teaching; it is not a human invention but the truth which God has revealed in and through Christ His Son.

From the first, the Apostles were called *Apostles,* a word which means "men who are sent," or "messengers." Nor is there any doubt who it is that sends them—it is Christ, the Master.

The Church Was Established as a Visible Society

It is clear from the Gospels that Christ intended His Church to be a visible society, that is, a social group that would be recognizable by the generality of men. It would not be an invisible reality consisting only of holy people, whose identity would be known only to God.

From the passage that deals with fraternal correction (Mt. 18), it is clear that the Church can be addressed ("tell it to the church") and the delinquent can be corrected authoritatively by the Church, so that if he refuses to accept her admonitions, he can be excommunicated: "If he refuses to listen even to the church, let him be to you as a Gentile and a tax collector" (18:17).

Persecutors would be able to identify those who belonged to Christ, and this could only be through their membership in a visible church (Mt. 5:11).

In several parables the kingdom of God has the lineaments of a visible society. The followers of Christ, who are to be the light of the world, will be like a city set on a hill and visible to all (Mt. 5:14). The net which is cast into the sea and gathers in good fish and also worthless has definite outlines—some fish are inside the line of bobbing corks and others outside; and the same is true of the field that has a mixed crop of wheat and tares—it may not be fenced, but it has well-defined limits, and the owner and his neighbors are well aware of these.

The word *Church* is found in the Gospel of Matthew, the Acts of the Apostles and the Epistles. It signifies "assembly" and corresponds to the Aramaic "Qahal." Like its Aramaic counterpart, it stands for a well-defined social group of which one becomes a member by a rite of initiation—in the case of the Jewish Qahal, circumcision; and for the Christian Church, Baptism.

Texts have been quoted by those who reject our thesis to prove that the Church is a purely spiritual reality whose members are known only to God, but these texts prove nothing of the kind. One such is Luke 17:20, 21: "The kingdom of God is not coming with signs to be observed-...for behold, the kingdom of God is in the midst of you."

With these words, Jesus rejected the demand of the Pharisees for a spectacular sign that would serve to inaugurate the kingdom of God. The kingdom of God, He declared, is already among them in its beginnings, but they have not recognized it. He was not saying that the kingdom is a purely interior reality, hidden in the heart of each individual man.

Another is John 4:21, 23: "The hour is coming when neither on this mountain nor in Jerusalem will you worship the Father.... But the hour is coming when true worshipers will worship the Father in spirit and truth, for such the Father seeks to worship him."

What Christ is saying here is that the worship of God will not be confined to one sanctuary, whether on Mt. Gerizim or on Mt. Sion, but will be worldwide, free from all restrictions of place or nation, and because of the removal of these restrictions, it will be more interior than that which is offered on Gerizim or Sion.

It has been argued that the Apostles would not have understood Christ's reference to the Church in Matthew 16 and 18 as referring to anything other than the Synagogue. To this we reply that however imperfectly the Apostles understood Christ's meaning at the time, they understood later that the Church of which Christ had spoken was to be distinct from the Synagogue.

The Church Is an Eschatological Society

Eschatology is concerned with "the last things"—the final denouement at the end of time when God's purposes in human history are made manifest and the just enter into eternal glory and the wicked into eternal misery.

The kingdom of God which Christ came to establish on earth looks forward to the Last Judgment, when the just shall shine like the sun (Mt. 13:43), and the Son of Man will come in His glory (Mt. 25:31). When the end will come has not been revealed: "Of that day or that hour no one knows, not even the angels in heaven, nor the Son, but only the Father" (Mk. 13:32). It will come when no one is expecting it: "But as to the times and the seasons, brethren, you have no need to have anything written to you. For you yourselves know well that the day of the Lord will come like a thief in the night" (1 Thes. 5:1-2).

There are some indications in the Gospels that the end is to come in a distant future. In the parable of the mustard seed, the tree is to extend its branches over the whole earth (Mt. 13:31); the nobleman in the parable of the wicked vinedressers (Lk. 20:9-16) is to go into a far country and tarry long; the Gospel must be preached to all nations (Mk. 13:10), even to the ends of the earth (Acts 1:8).

With the creation of the Church, the human race has entered upon the final era in its history. Its members are they "upon whom the end of the ages has come" (1 Cor. 10:11). It is right therefore to describe the present time as the age of "inaugurated eschatology." In this intermediate period the kingdom will contain a mixture of good men and bad. The field in which the landholder has sown good seed will also contain tares which have been sown by the Evil One; the net will pull in not only good fish but also worthless ones, and the sorting out will be done only at the end of the world; and it is only at the end that the sheep will be separated from the goats (Mt. 25).

Christ makes a clear distinction between this present time when His followers will be persecuted and the time of reward, and He promises His assistance in this present time, until the end comes (Mt. 28:20).

Some scholars have maintained that Christ thought the end of the world was close at hand. They quote His words: "Truly, I say to you, this generation will not pass away till all these things take place" (Mt. 24:34). The reference is not perfectly clear, but it seems He was speaking of the fall of Jerusalem.

Some Rationalist critics (e.g., J. Weiss, Schweitzer, Loisy) have gone so far as to maintain that the nearness of the end of the world was the central theme of Jesus' preaching.

They have chosen a few texts which *could* bear this interpretation and neglected the others which point to a long period before the end comes. In His discourse on the last things (Mt. 24) Jesus makes a distinction between the destruction of Jerusalem, which is to happen within a generation and will be preceded by signs portending the event, and the end of the world, which will come suddenly like lightning out of a cloudless sky.

It seems that the first generation of Christians hoped that the end would come soon and were of the opinion that it would, but the Apostles refrained from asserting categorically that it would. St. Peter does indeed say that "the end of all things is at hand" (1 Pt. 4:7), but these words are in the context of moral exhortation and retain their force, since the world ends for each man when he dies, and death is no distant prospect for any man alive.

Christ Instituted His Church as a Structured Society, Governed by a Hierarchy

It is clear from the Gospels that Christ did not leave His disciples an unorganized crowd, but established a hierarchical order among them.

In the first place, He chose the Twelve, and kept them with Him constantly.

It was they who distributed the food at the feeding of the five thousand, and they who argued about pre-eminence among their number—who was to have the first place in the kingdom. It was to them that Jesus promised that they would sit on twelve thrones judging the twelve tribes of Israel, but first they must be "fishers of men." They would teach with His authority—"he that listens to you listens to me"; and they would share His sufferings.

The earliest written reference to "the twelve" dates from 55 A.D., when 1 Corinthians was written: "He appeared to Cephas and then to the twelve" (15:5).

In the Gospels Judas Iscariot is often designated as "one of the twelve." While the phrase emphasizes what was painful and scandalous in the fact that it was one of the privileged disciples that betrayed the Master, the formula attests at the same time the existence of the group of the Twelve before the Passion. Not that there is any doubt about the fact, for the Synoptic Gospels contain many references to "the twelve," "the twelve disciples," "the twelve apostles."

The Twelve were not elected by the body of the faithful, as they would be in a democracy, but they were chosen directly by Christ Himself, and they received their authority from Him.

The choice is described as proceeding from Christ alone: "And he went up into the hills, and called to him those whom he desired; and they came to him. And he appointed twelve, to be with him, and to be sent out to preach and have authority to cast out demons: Simon, whom he surnamed Peter..." (Mk. 3:13-16).

This group is clearly distinguished from the seventy others whom Christ sent out on a specific mission (Lk. 10:1), and who seem to have disbanded as soon as the mission was accomplished. Jesus asserted that He had chosen the Twelve freely: "Did I not choose you, the twelve" (Jn. 6:70), and again: "You did not choose me, but I chose you" (Jn. 15:16). In this He differed from the ordinary rabbi, whom the pupils chose as their master. He identifies their mission with His: "As you sent me into the world, so I have sent them into the world" (Jn. 17:18), and again, "As the Father has sent me, even so I send you" (Jn. 20:21).

The title of Apostle was given to the Twelve by Christ Himself: "And when it was day, he called his disciples and chose from them twelve, whom he named apostles" (Lk. 6:13).

The term was applied also to those who were chosen directly by Christ Himself after His resurrection, whether through the casting of lots, as in the case of Matthias (Acts 1:24-26) or by an extraordinary intervention, as in the case of Paul (Gal. 1:1). But after his call, Paul had to be baptized; he sought the approbation of Peter, and had hands imposed on him when he was set aside for the mission to the Gentiles (Acts 9:6, 17; 13:2, 3; Gal. 1:18; 2:2). This may be the reason why St. Paul made a distinction between himself and those whom he called the "superlative apostles" (2 Cor. 11:5).

The term "apostle" was also used in a wider sense to designate emissaries of local churches like Epaphroditus (Phil. 2:28) or the apostles of the churches (2 Cor. 8:23). But there is no doubt that in the strict sense the term was reserved for the members of the apostolic college, "the twelve," the twelve apostles of the Lamb, whose names are on the foundations of the New Jerusalem (Apoc. 21:14).

Conscious of the authority they have received from Christ, the Twelve begin at once after Pentecost to govern the new society of those who have come to believe in Christ. They are named individually (Acts 1:13) and the number is brought up to twelve by the choice of Matthias.

After the manner of the Jewish Sanhedrin, they govern the infant Church, teach with authority and determine the manner of worship. There is no challenge to their authority. The others listen, obey, and cling to the rites they have determined. Sinners are castigated (Acts 5:3-11), and the authority of the Jewish Sanhedrin is resisted when it attempts to put a stop to the preaching of the Resurrection.

The Infallible Teaching Authority of the Apostles

The Apostles taught authoritatively what they had been taught by Christ and they were certain that, thanks to the assistance of the Holy Spirit, promised at the Last Supper and given at Pentecost, what they taught was true.

Infallibility is the prerogative enjoyed by those who in their teaching are preserved from error by the action of the Holy Spirit. This is the assistance promised by Christ when He declared that He would be with His Church until the end of time (Mt. 28:20), and it is essential if those who accept the teaching of the Apostles and their successors are to be sure that what they are being taught is the truth revealed by God.

Infallibility is not to be reduced to indefectibility, or the continuance of the Church in existence, as Hans Küng has maintained.[7] If the Church were not infallible in her teaching, she could authoritatively proclaim as true what in fact is false. If this took place, she would lose her identity and no longer be the Church which Christ founded. Küng's novel interpretation of infallibility is based on an erroneous conception of the Church, as if she were an ill-defined mass, consisting of all those who in some fashion profess their faith in Christ. This conception, as we have seen, has no basis in the New Testament texts.

Christ came as one sent by the Father to expound with authority the hidden mysteries of the kingdom of God (Col. 1:26; Eph. 1:9), testifying to what He knew by direct vision: "Truly, truly, I say to you, we speak of what we know, and bear witness to what we have seen" (Jn. 3:11).

As the Word Incarnate, He conveyed to men, by His teaching, His life, His death and resurrection, the message that had been entrusted to Him by His Father. "My teaching," He declared, "is not mine, but his who sent me" (Jn. 7:16).

He came to bear witness to the truth (Jn. 18:37) and He did this by His teaching and His death on the cross

(1 Tm. 6:13). To carry on this work of bearing witness to the truth of God, He commissioned His Apostles: "All authority in heaven and on earth has been given to me. Go therefore and make disciples of all nations, baptizing them in the name of the Father and of the Son and of the Holy Spirit, teaching them to observe all that I have commanded you; and lo, I am with you always, to the close of the age" (Mt. 28:18-20).

Those who hear the Apostles will be morally obliged to accept their teaching, just as those who heard Christ were morally obliged to accept His teaching: "He who hears you hears me, and he who rejects you rejects me, and he who rejects me rejects him who sent me" (Lk. 10:16).

To fulfill this obligation, these hearers will need the help of God, whether it be to accept the teaching of Christ or of His Apostles. "He who is of God hears the words of God" (Jn. 8:47), and the same is true of those who accept the teaching of the Apostles: "Whoever knows God listens to us, and he who is not of God does not listen to us" (1 Jn. 4:6).

In several places in the New Testament (Acts 13:46; 1 Thes. 2:13; Heb. 13:7) the Gospel message is called "the word of God."

This is a Jewish phrase, which implies infallibility, for the word of God, coming from the prophets and written in Scripture, cannot but be true.

The Apostles, knowing they enjoyed the guidance of the Holy Spirit, claimed infallibility for their preaching. To this guidance they appealed when they formulated their decree that the Gentiles were no longer bound by the Mosaic Law: "It has seemed good to the Holy Spirit and to us to lay upon you no greater burden than this..." (Acts 15:28).

St. Paul speaks of the wisdom he preaches as having been revealed to him by the Holy Spirit, who searches everything, even the depths of God (1 Cor. 2:10, 13), and he is so sure of the truth of what he has taught the Galatians that he excludes with an anathema any different teaching, even if it were brought to them by an angel (Gal. 1:8-9). In another place (2 Cor. 13:3), he asserts that it is Christ who is speaking in him.

From the earliest times it has been a basic principle of Christian thought that the Apostles were infallible in their proclamation of the truths revealed by God.

In the second century, the Gnostic heretics claimed that their teachings came from the Apostles, being a secret doctrine different from that which they had taught publicly. St. Irenaeus rejected the Gnostic claim and maintained that if we wish to know what the Apostles taught we must turn to their successors, the bishops of the Catholic Church. But both St. Irenaeus and his Gnostic adversaries agreed that if we are to know with certainty what God has revealed, we must turn to the teaching of the Apostles.

In the third century the great scholar Origen wrote: "Let there be kept the ecclesiastical preaching handed down by the Apostles through the order of succession and abiding in the Church to this day: only that truth is to be believed which is wholly in harmony with the ecclesiastical and apostolic tradition." [8]

When a Council of the Church defines some article of the Faith it declares that it does so in order to safeguard the truth that was taught by the Apostles. Thus St. Athanasius, writing in the fourth century, tells us that the bishops at the Council of Nicaea, when they defined that the Son is consubstantial with the Father, declared that this is what the Catholic Church believes, and they went on to say that this doctrine was not of recent origin, but is apostolic, so that they were inventing nothing but teaching the same truth as the Apostles taught. [9]

In our own day the Second Vatican Council declared that there is continuity between the teaching of the bishops of today and the teaching of the Apostles: "Among those various offices which have been exercised in the Church from the earliest times, the chief place, according to the witness of tradition, is held by the function of those who, through their appointment to the dignity and responsibility of bishop, and in virtue consequently of the unbroken succession going back to the beginning, are regarded as transmitters of the apostolic line. Thus, according to the testimony of St. Irenaeus, the apostolic tradition is manifested and preserved in the whole world by those who were made bishops by the Apostles and by their successors down to our own time." [10]

Authority To Govern the Church

In every social group, someone must exercise authority if the group is not to disintegrate, and the Church, as a visible society, is not an exception to this rule. In the state, this authority may be vested in a monarch or in an elected parliament. In the Church, this authority, called the power of jurisdiction, was given to the Twelve, entitling them to make laws, to pass judgment on those who infringed these laws, and to inflict punishment on the guilty.

As we have seen, the Apostles exercised their legislative power at the Council of Jerusalem (Acts 15). They had been prepared for this role by Christ when He told them that anything they bound or loosed on earth would be bound or loosed in heaven (Mt. 18:18). "Binding and loosing" is a rabbinical expression and it signifies the authority to forbid or allow certain kinds of behavior, that is, to make genuine laws. The same power was promised to Peter individually at Caesarea Philippi (Mt. 16:19).

This authority was not given to all the disciples, but only to the Twelve, and it was to be exercised by them, not in any absolutist fashion, but in dependence on Christ and in conformity with His teaching (Mt. 28:19-20).

In the New Testament we find instances of the Apostles passing judgment on offenders and inflicting punishment on them. St. Paul, for example, passed judgment on the incestuous man (1 Cor. 5:1-2) and we find him excommunicating Hymenaeus and Alexander, handing them over "to the power of Satan," in order that this chastisement might bring them to a better frame of mind (2 Tm. 2:17-19).

St. Peter condemned Ananias and Sapphira for asserting fraudulently that they had given all their goods to the community; and God confirmed the Apostle's judgment by striking the offenders dead (Acts 5:1-11).

St. Paul threatened to deal with some recalcitrants in Corinth: "If I come again I will not spare them.... I write this while I am away from you, in order that when I come I may not have to be severe in my use of the authority which the Lord has given me for building up and not for tearing down" (2 Cor. 13:2, 10).

By thus governing the Church, the Apostles were acting in accordance with the instructions of Christ, who clearly taught that His Church would have the power to excommunicate: "If he refuses to listen to the church, let him be to you as a Gentile and a tax collector" (Mt. 18:17). Since a Jew should not associate with a Gentile or a tax collector, Christ is here ordering that he who refuses to submit to the authority of the Church is to be expelled from the community.

The Power of Order

Christ established the Church to glorify the Father by the sanctification of His disciples, and this she does by proclaiming the truths which God has revealed, making laws to foster holiness of life and engaging in worship with the use of external rites.

Under the Old Law, ceremonial worship was very important, indeed the central feature of the Jewish religion. Christ approved of the Jewish ritual, though He distinguished between what was of merely human origin and what was prescribed in Holy Scripture, and He Himself faithfully observed the prescriptions of the Law. He went to Jerusalem at the age of twelve, He celebrated the great Jewish feasts and worshiped in the Synagogue.

However, it was His intention to establish a new covenant, and with it a new manner of worshiping God, which would be more spiritual and not limited to a single locality.

He prescribed Baptism (Mk. 16:16; Mt. 28:19; Jn. 3:5), and He Himself baptized (Jn. 3:22, 26). He prescribed the reception of the Eucharist (Jn. 6:53), and at the Last Supper instituted the Eucharistic sacrifice, which, as Malachi had foretold (1:11), was to be offered throughout the world.

To the Apostles He gave the power to consecrate the Eucharist with the words: "Do this in remembrance of me" (Lk. 22:19), and the power to forgive sins when He breathed on them and said: "Receive the Holy Spirit. If you forgive the sins of any, they are forgiven; if you retain the sins of any, they are retained" (Jn. 20:22-23).

On the day of Pentecost the Apostles baptized three thousand, and it was by means of this rite that those who believed in Christ were made members of the Church.

They celebrated the Eucharist, a rite referred to as "the breaking of bread" (Acts 2:46; 20:7) and alluded to in sacrificial terms in 1 Corinthians 10:14-22.[11]

Our information about the half century that followed the composition of the Acts of the Apostles is scanty, but about the year 110 we find St. Ignatius of Antioch stating that it is the bishop who consecrates the Eucharist.[12]

Conclusion

Christ came into the world to establish a new covenant between God and His people, to found a new religion, bringing to completion the process which had begun with the call of Abraham. Revealing truths barely hinted at in earlier times, proposing a moral code that was more demanding than that of Moses, and instituting a new mode of worship in which there was no place for the slaughter of animals, He provided for the execution of His grand design by establishing the Church as a visible society hierarchically organized and promising her the assistance of the Holy Spirit until the end of time.

This Church, whose early history is recorded in the Acts of the Apostles and touched on unsystematically in the Epistles of St. Paul, has persisted through the centuries and is in fact the only institution that has survived from the far-off days when Tiberius was governing the Roman Empire. As at her beginning, so throughout the intervening centuries, she has authoritatively taught the truths expounded by her Divine Founder, upheld the moral law He promulgated, and worshiped God with the rites which He instituted.

Of this Church the Second Vatican Council spoke when it said: "This is the sole Church of Christ which in the Creed we profess to be one, holy, catholic and apostolic, which our Savior after His resurrection entrusted to Peter's pastoral care (Jn. 21:17), commissioning him and the other Apostles to extend and rule it (cf. Mt. 28:18ff.), and which He raised up for all ages as 'the pillar and mainstay of the truth' (1 Tm. 3:15). This Church, constituted and organized as a society in the present world, subsists in the Catholic Church, which is governed by the successor of Peter and by the bishops in communion with him." [13]

Within the Church the institution most easily discernible as that which links the Church of today with the Church of Apostolic times is the Roman papacy—the unbroken line of the bishops of the Roman See, extending from St. Peter to Pope John Paul II. To its New Testament credentials we must now turn our attention.

Notes

1. R. McBrien, *Catholicism,* Dove Publications, Melbourne, 1980, p. 717.
2. *Dogmatic Constitution on the Church (Lumen gentium),* no. 8.
3. *De Controversiis Christianae Fidei,* Vol. II, Bk. 3, Ch. 2.
4. Letter to the Smyrnaeans, no. 8, in *Early Christian Writings,* (tr. Maxwell Staniforth), Penguin Books, Ltd., London, 1968, (p. 121.
5. *The Martyrdom of Polycarp,* no. 16, *ibid.,* p. 161.
6. Book V, ch. 13.
7. *Infallible? An Enquiry* (tr. Eric Mosbacher), Collins, London, 1971.
8. *Peri Archon,* I, 1, no. 2, PG 11:116.
9. *Epistula de Synodis,* no. 5, PG 26:688.
10. *Dogmatic Constitution on the Church (Lumen Gentium),* no. 20.
11. Cf. Cardinal Shehan, art. "The Priest in the New Testament: Another Point of View" in *The Homiletic and Pastoral Review,* New York, November,. 1975.

12. *Letter to the Smyrnaeans,* no. 8, in *Early Christian Writings.*

13. *Dogmatic Constitution on the Church (Lumen Gentium),* no. 8.

References

A. de Bovis, S.J., *The Church, Christ's Mystery and Sacrament,* Burns and Oates (Faith and Fact Books, no. 48), London, 1961.

M. D'Herbigny, S.J., *Theologica De Ecclesia,* Beauchesne, Paris, 2 Vols., 1927-1928.

Ch. Journet, *The Church of the Word Incarnate* (tr. A. H. C. Downes), Sheed and Ward, London, 1955.

H. De Lubac, S.J., *The Church, Paradox and Mystery* (tr. James H. Dunne), Ecclesia Press, Shannon, 1969.

R. Schnackenburg, *The Church in the New Testament* (tr. W. J. O'Hara), Seabury, New York, 1965.

VIII. The Primacy of the Roman Pontiff

The Primacy of Peter

Christ intended to establish a Church that would endure until He returned to judge the world. How would He enable it to withstand the buffetings to which every institution in the world is subject and remain in being throughout the ages? "The wise man," He had declared in the Sermon on the Mount, "builds on rock" (Mt. 7:24). So when He came to build His Church, He chose one man, Simon the son of John, and giving him a new name, "Cephas," which is Aramaic for rock, made him the bedrock on which the foundations of the Church were to rest.

It is sometimes thought that the Catholic case for the primacy of Peter rests almost wholly on the promise made at Caesarea Philippi (Mt. 16:18-20), but this is not so. The text is indeed a capital one, but even without it there is ample evidence in the Gospels to show that Christ intended Peter to be the head of His Church, and this is corroborated by Peter's behavior as recorded in the Acts of the Apostles.

The Evidence of the Gospels

At His first meeting with Peter, Christ told him he would be given a new name, "Cephas" (Jn. 1:42). Among the Semites, the name has great significance, and when

God bestows a new name on some individual, as He did for Abraham (Gn. 17:5), this is to indicate that he will play an important part in the fulfillment of God's designs. When St. Luke comes to list the twelve Apostles (6:14-16), he puts at the head of the list, "Simon, whom he named Peter," and when the list of the Apostles is given elsewhere (Mt. 10:2-4; Mk. 3:14-19; Acts 1:13), although there is some variation in the order of the other names, Peter's name always heads the list: Peter is "the first" (Mt. 10:2). Peter gives his name to the whole group: "Simon and those who were with him" (Mk. 1:36). It is the same idiom as is found in the passage in Acts (5:17): "The high priest rose up and all who were with him, that is, the party of the Sadducees."

His name comes first, too, when the inner group of Peter, James and John is named (e.g., as in the account of the Transfiguration, Mt. 17:1).

Peter acts as leader and spokesman of the Apostolic group, and is so regarded by others, like the officials who came to collect the Temple tax (Mt. 17:24-27). This tax was a half-shekel, to be paid by the head of every household. Peter, acting on Christ's orders, went to catch a fish with a shekel in its mouth. This coin would pay for the tax twice over, and it was to be given to the collectors, Christ said, "for me and for yourself." In this way He made it clear that, after Himself, Peter was the head of the little group.

Christ made Peter's house His headquarters when He settled in Capernaum (Mk. 1:29); He taught from Peter's boat and it was in Peter's net that the great haul of fish was taken (Lk. 5:1-11). The discussion about who was to be the greatest in the kingdom of heaven (Mk. 9:33-37) was almost certainly prompted by Christ's choice of Peter as leader.

In His training of the Apostles, Christ showed special solicitude for Peter, instructing and correcting him and enabling him by a miracle to walk upon the water (Mt. 14:28-33).

At the Last Supper Christ clearly indicates that Peter is to have a special role among the Twelve. The Apostles have been arguing about precedence, and this leads the Master to stress the need for humility. He then goes on to say that Satan will strive to win the Twelve to His cause, but His scheme will be thwarted because Christ has prayed specially for Peter. In the course of the Passion, Peter will deny his Master, but after his conversion his firmness in the faith will preserve the faith of his companions: "Simon, Simon, behold, Satan demanded to have you [i.e., the Twelve], that he might sift you like wheat, but I have prayed for you [i.e., Simon] that your faith may not fail; and when you have turned again, strengthen your brethren" (Lk. 22:31-32).

Commenting on this passage, Ethelbert Stauffer, a Lutheran scholar, writes: "What is the basis of Peter's unique position? Not upon any special qualification of the Apostle, but upon the intercession of the Lord. The adversary intends to destroy the people of God, and he will have much success, but Jesus appears as an advocate against the accuser. But Jesus does not appeal for His followers as a whole, but (and this is the surprising thing in the passage quoted above) for Peter. In praying specially for Peter, Jesus is protecting and delivering the young community as a whole. He prays for fallen Peter so that Peter uplifted might strengthen his brethren in the faith, and so all attain the goal reserved for them—the kingdom. So in this one saying it is made clear that the only possible ground of the Church's existence and the very basis of its life is the mediatorial office of Christ, and also that Peter's own mediatorial function is to be coordinated with and subordinated to this Christological office of the mediator." [1]

Peter occupies a special place in the New Testament accounts of the Resurrection. The holy women are bidden to go and tell His disciples and Peter that the Lord is risen (Mk. 16:7). The disciples returning from Emmaus are told that "the Lord has risen indeed, and has appeared to Simon" (Lk. 24:34). St. Paul, repeating the early tradition, writes: "He appeared to Cephas, and then to the twelve" (1 Cor. 15:5).

Commenting on this passage Stauffer writes: "According to 1 Corinthians 15:5, Peter was the first person to receive a *revelation* of the risen Christ. But in that passage, to receive a revelation is to be given an appointment (cf. 1 Cor. 15:5ff., with Gal. 1:16; 2:8). Therefore the emphasis on Peter being the first to receive a revelation is certain to involve a special appointment and a special task."[2]

The evidence we have just considered would suffice to show that Christ intended Peter to be the head of the Apostolic group. Should any doubts remain, they are removed when we take account of the very explicit testimony of the Gospels that Christ promised the primacy to Peter at Caesarea Philippi and conferred it on him after the Resurrection.

The Promise of the Primacy to Peter

Peter's profession of faith in Christ and the promise of the primacy (Mt. 16:13-28) came at a turning point in the public ministry of Christ. The preaching of the Good News in Galilee is at an end; from this time forward Jesus will concentrate His attention on forming the Twelve as He makes His way to Jerusalem, where His passion awaits Him.

The passage in which Peter is promised the primacy forms a close-knit whole. First comes the question: "Who do men say that the Son of Man is?" and then "Who do you say that I am?" Peter replies, acknowledging that Jesus is the Son of God and the long-awaited Messiah. The Master responds to Peter's profession of faith by promising him the primacy. Then He goes on to explain that His Messianic mission involves suffering and death. To this somber prospect Peter reacts all too humanly, urging Jesus to dismiss these forebodings as unfounded. He is rebuked sharply for his opposition to God's designs: "Get behind me, Satan, you are a hindrance to me; for you are not on the side of God, but of men." Jesus then goes on to state the general principle—all those who would follow Him must take up the cross and be prepared, even at the cost of life itself, to profess their faith in Him. Only thus can they hope to share in His glory.[3]

The words that concern us here are found in verses 17-19, "And Jesus answered him: 'Blessed are you, Simon Bar-Jona! For flesh and blood has not revealed this to you, but my Father who is in heaven. And I tell you, you are Peter, and on this rock I will build my church, and the powers of death shall not prevail against it. I will give you the keys of the kingdom of heaven, and whatever you bind on earth shall be bound in heaven, and whatever you loose on earth shall be loosed in heaven."

It is certain that this passage belongs to the Gospel of St. Matthew and was not interpolated by a later hand. It is found in all the MSS and there is no trace of the questioning that would have occurred had it been interpolated. Harnack indeed argued for interpolation, but his view has won few adherents.

St. Justin alludes to it in his *Dialogue with Trypho the Jew,*[4] as does St. Irenaeus in his *Adversus Haereses.*[5] It is cited in its entirety by Tatian in his *Diatessaron*[6] and by Tertullian in his *De Praescriptione haereticorum.*[7]

During the debates between the orthodox and their heretical adversaries the authenticity of the passage was taken by both parties as being above suspicion.

The genuineness of the passage emerges clearly from a study of the text itself. "The great antiquity and Palestinian origin of this passage," Cullmann writes, "may today be considered beyond doubt."[8]

The phrases used and the structure of v. 18—three lines of three strophes each—are typically Aramaic.

"Simon Bar-Jona" is a typically Aramaic designation; and the phrases "flesh and blood," "building a church," "the gates of hell," "the keys of the kingdom of heaven" and "binding and loosing" are likewise typically Aramaic. There is no trace of such idioms as these in Greek.

It is certain that the words: "You are Peter, and on this rock I will build my church" signify that it is on Peter personally that the Church will be built. Alternative explanations, e.g., that "this rock" referred to Christ, or to

Peter's faith, or his profession of faith, were advanced by Protestant polemicists in earlier times, but these have now been abandoned. T. G. Jalland quotes Stevens, a modern Protestant writer, to this effect: "It is quite certain, and is now generally admitted, that the words 'this rock' refer, not to Christ, nor to Peter's confession of faith, but to Peter himself."[9]

The three metaphorical expressions used by Christ in v. 18 signify both supreme teaching authority and a primacy of jurisdiction, i.e., supreme governing authority.

1. Peter is to be the rock on which the Church is to be built. A building that has its foundations on bedrock will not be overwhelmed by storms. So the Church built on Peter will derive from him stability and unity. It will never die or be overthrown by the powers of evil, intent as these are on leading the whole Church into error.

What foundation on rock is for a building, supreme authority is for a society—a source of unity and stability. Hence in promising to make Peter the rock on which the Church will be built Christ promises him supreme authority to teach and thereby maintain the unity of Faith, and supreme authority to govern—to make laws which all must obey and see that they are obeyed. The spiritual society that is to come into being will be a monarchy.

2. Peter is to be the bearer of the keys of the kingdom of heaven. His role is like that of the Keeper of the Seal or the Chancellor, who is first in the kingdom after the king. Peter will have the right to determine who may enter the kingdom and who is to be excluded (cf. Is. 22:22; Apoc. 3:7).

3. Peter will have the power to impose obligations and to do away with them, that is he will have supreme legislative, judicial and coercive power.

What is promised here to Peter personally will be promised to the whole Apostolic college in Matthew 18:18, but this in no way detracts from the uniqueness of Peter's role.

The foundation is essential for the existence of the city of God, and the power of the keys for its security, but the power of binding and loosing, which is essential to life within the city can be exercised collegially, as it was by the judiciary in Imperial Russia, where, nevertheless, supreme authority was vested in the Czar.

The principal objection brought against the genuineness of Matthew 16:18 is that it contains the word "church," which is not found elsewhere in the Gospels except in Matthew 18:17.

Those who hold that Christ only proclaimed the coming of the kingdom in the immediate future and had no idea of founding a Church, naturally maintain that He could not have used the word.

This objection is based on the erroneous idea that Christ had no intention of founding a Church. It loses much of its force when we see that if the word "church" is lacking elsewhere in the Gospels, references to the reality are not. St. John, for example, does not use the word in his Gospel, but he portrays Christ as the Shepherd, and His flock cannot but be the Church.

The Conferring of the Primacy

St. John tells us in the last chapter of his Gospel how the primacy promised to Peter at Caesarea Philippi was conferred on him. After the Resurrection the Apostles return to Galilee. They go fishing and after a night of fruitless toil they draw near to the shore where Jesus, whom they have not yet recognized, is waiting for them. Following His directions they make a large haul of fish. They then come ashore and eat the meal which Jesus has prepared for them. The meal over, Jesus addresses Peter: "Simon, son of John, do you love me more than these?" Peter makes no claim to a greater love and replies simply: "Yes, Lord, you know that I love you." The question is repeated three times, and each time Peter replies, affirming his love for the Master, thereby making amends for his threefold denial during the Passion. After each reply, Jesus bids him tend, first the lambs, then the older sheep, and finally the whole flock: "Feed my lambs, feed my sheep."

In many places in the Old Testament the Messiah is portrayed as a shepherd having Israel as His flock (cf. Mic. 5:2-5; Is. 40:11; Jer. 23:2-4; Ez. 34; 37:24).

When therefore Christ declared: "I am the good shepherd" (Jn. 10:14) He was making a Messianic claim; and the same claim is implicit in the statement that He was sent to the lost sheep of the house of Israel (Mt. 15:24).

Now that He is glorified He remains "the great shepherd of the flock" (cf. Heb. 13:20; 1 Pt. 5:4), but before His Ascension He decided to make Peter His vicar on earth. Peter is to be the shepherd of the whole flock. It will be his task to see that the sheep are fed sound doctrine and guided along the path of holiness. And although he must exercise his authority with humility, he must possess this authority, since without it he could not fulfill his shepherd's role.

It is to be noted that the words were addressed to Peter alone. The other Apostles present were merely witnesses of this solemn investiture with power. John, who was one of them, was greatly loved by Jesus, but there is never any suggestion that anyone but Peter was the leader.

Peter as Head of the Infant Church

After the Ascension the rivalries that marked the public ministry are a thing of the past; all acknowledge Peter as head of the little group.

The first twelve chapters of the Acts are full of the doings of Peter. It is he, as head of the 120 who were gathered in prayer before Pentecost, who urges that another be selected to replace Judas in the Twelve, and sets out the conditions this person must fulfill to be recognized as an Apostle (Acts 1:15-26). He is the first to preach to the crowd at Pentecost, exhorting them to repent and be baptized in the name of Christ (2:14-40). He is the first to work a miracle, curing the lame man at the Beautiful Gate of the Temple (3:1-10), and people put their sick out into the streets so that Peter's shadow might fall on them (5:15-16).

Peter is the instrument of God's vengeance on Ananias and Sapphira (5:1-11). He goes with John to Samaria to confirm the believers there, and in that city he rejects Simon Magus' offer of money as the price of spiritual powers (8:9-24).

At Joppa he raises Tabitha from the dead (9:36-41) and it is there he has the mysterious vision of the sheet containing clean and unclean animals, teaching him that salvation is now being offered to pagans as well as Jews (10:1-48). He speaks first at the Council of Jerusalem, arguing that the Law of Moses should not be imposed on converts from paganism.

Objections

1. It has been argued that because Peter and John were sent by the Jerusalem community to Samaria (Acts 8:14), Peter could not have been head of the Church.

Reply. Prior discussion and the backing of the group of which one is the head do not imply that one has no authority over the group. The mission to Samaria was a delicate one, for it was a question of admitting the hated Samaritans to the new community, and Peter and John went, with the backing of the community, as its most authoritative members.

2. In Antioch, Peter, to conciliate the Jewish Christians, gave up eating with the Gentile Christians, and he was rebuked by Paul (Gal. 2:11-14). Some have argued that this implies that Paul did not recognize Peter as head of the Church.

Reply. Paul rebuked Peter because his behavior was a source of scandal to the faithful and contrary to the principle that he had enunciated at the conversion of Cornelius (cf. Acts 10:28) and at the Council of Jerusalem (15:9). Because of Peter's pre-eminence, other Jewish Christians, and even Barnabas, followed his example. This division of the community would have been ruinous, and the Gentile Christians could have gathered that it was necessary to follow the Jewish regulations about meals.

In rebuking Peter, Paul was fulfilling his duty of fraternal correction, not contesting Peter's authority, which Paul had acknowledged when he went up to Jerusalem three years after his conversion (Gal. 1:18).

Commenting on this incident, St. Thomas writes: "Where the faith is publicly endangered, prelates are to be publicly rebuked. Hence Paul, who was subject to Peter, publicly rebuked him on account of the imminent danger to the faith through scandal." [10]

The Primacy of the Roman Pontiff

The Sole Claim of the Bishop of Rome

Until the schism of the 11th Century brought about the break between Rome and Constantinople which still endures, the whole Church acknowledged the Bishop of Rome as its head. He, and he alone, has claimed to be the Successor of St. Peter and by this title to have the right to exercise jurisdiction over the whole Church.

The Claim Recognized in the First Century

The claims of the Roman Pontiff in our day are no more extensive than those made by Pope Leo the Great in the Fifth Century, who wrote: "Through the most blessed Peter, chief of the Apostles, the holy Roman Church holds the principate over all the Churches of the whole world." [11]

In 451, the Council of Chalcedon acknowledged that Pope Leo had authority to determine doctrine for the whole Church and accepted the *Tome* in which he set out the Catholic faith regarding the mystery of the Incarnation.

But long before the Fifth Century, the Bishops of Rome had exercised this primacy over the whole Church. Indeed, Harnack, the great Protestant historian, has stated that Rome exercised a factual primacy from early in the Second Century. [12]

Many documents pertaining to these early centuries have been lost. The archives of the Church of Rome, for example, were destroyed during the persecution of Diocletian at the beginning of the Fourth Century.[13] There is, however, ample evidence from the preceding centuries of the pre-eminence of the Roman See.

The Letter of St. Clement

In an Epistle which is usually dated 96 A.D., but may well have been written in 70, St. Clement, writing on behalf of the Church of Rome, exhorted the Christians of Corinth to put an end to their quarrels and reinstate some presbyters who had been unlawfully deposed.[14] The Roman church writes with authority: "There must be no time lost in putting an end to this state of affairs," and again, "If there are any who refuse to heed the declarations He has made through our lips, let them not doubt the gravity of the guilt and the peril in which they involve themselves."[15]

Clement takes for granted that the Church of Rome has the right to call a sister church to order; and his admonitions were received with such reverence that for the next two centuries his Epistle was read on Sundays in the liturgy together with the books of the New Testament.

Letter of St. Ignatius of Antioch

St. Ignatius of Antioch, when on his way to Rome where he suffered martyrdom about the year 110, addressed letters to six churches, including the Church of Rome. This letter begins with a greeting of extraordinary solemnity: "To her who has found mercy in the greatness of the All-Highest Father and Jesus Christ His only Son; to the church beloved and enlightened in her love of our God Jesus Christ by the will of Him who wills all things; to the church holding chief place in the territories of the districts of Rome—worthy of honor, blessing, praise and success; worthy too in holiness, foremost in love, observing the law of Christ and bearing the Father's name. Greetings in the name of Jesus Christ. All perfect happiness in Jesus Christ our God, to you who are bodily and spiritually at one with all His commandments, fulfilled with the grace of God, and purified from every alien and discoloring stain." There is a striking difference between this and the greeting addressed to the Church of Tralles: "To the holy church in Tralles in Asia; beloved of God the Father of Jesus Christ, elect and godly, endowed with peace of body and soul by the passion of Jesus Christ, who through our rising again in Him is our Hope. In apostolic fashion I send the church my greetings in all the fullness of God, and wish her every happiness."

There is much argument about the exact meaning of the greeting addressed to the Romans. Some say that the phrase about presiding refers to a presidency over the whole Church; others hold that it has to do only with the territory around Rome. What is certain is that for Ignatius the Church of Rome had a certain pre-eminence.

St. Polycarp

St. Polycarp, the bishop of Smyrna, who had been a disciple of St. John the Apostle, came to Rome when he was in his 80's to discuss with Pope St. Anicetus (154-166) the question of the date on which Easter should be celebrated. He did not adopt the Roman custom, but he and the Pope parted amicably. This long journey at an advanced age indicates that for Polycarp the Church of Rome had a special place in the Christian scheme of things.

St. Irenaeus

St. Irenaeus, a disciple of Polycarp, who came to Rome and later became bishop of Lyons, is a witness to the primitive tradition of the Church in the East and West. In his book *Adversus Haereses* he has a famous passage that bears witness to the pre-eminence of the Roman See. Arguing against the Gnostic heretics, who claimed to have received secret doctrines not available to the ordinary Christian, Irenaeus maintained that the sure way of discovering what God has revealed is to have recourse to the churches which were founded by the Apostles and have preserved their teaching intact. Then he adds: "Since, however, it would be very tedious, in such a volume as this, to reckon up all the successions of all the churches, we do put to confusion all those who, in whatever manner, whether by an evil self-pleasing, by vainglory, by blindness and perverse opinion, assemble in unauthorized meetings; [we do this, I say] by indicating that tradition derived from the Apostles, of the very great, the very ancient and universally known Church founded and organized at Rome by the two most glorious Apostles, Peter and Paul; as also [by pointing out] the faith preached to men, which comes down to our own time by means of the successions of the bishops. For it is a matter of necessity that every Church should agree with this Church, on account of its preeminent authority, that is the faithful everywhere, inasmuch as the apostolic tradition has been preserved continuously by these [faithful men] who exist everywhere."[16]

The exact meaning of this passage has been much discussed, but it is clear that for Irenaeus, an individual or a local church which disagrees with Rome by that fact departs from the apostolic tradition and the unity of faith.

In 177, when Irenaeus was still a priest, he brought letters to Pope St. Eleutherius from the martyrs in Lyons, asking him to provide a remedy for the disturbances which the Montanists were causing in Lyons.

St. Victor

Some years later, being then bishop of Lyons, he wrote to Pope St. Victor (189-197), urging him not to excommunicate the churches of the East who were clinging to their custom of beginning their celebration of the Easter mysteries on the 14th Nisan, which might or might not be a Friday. Irenaeus did not contest Victor's right to excommunicate the eastern bishops, but he pointed out that six of Victor's predecessors had tolerated the Eastern usage. The view of Irenaeus—that Victor was not exceeding his powers—was the general view. Jalland writes: "There is no trace of a protest against Victor's action on grounds of principle. No one suggested that he had not the right to act as he had done."[17]

During the second century there was a constant stream of religious teachers to Rome. Catholics came there to be strengthened in the faith, and heretics in the hope of winning the support of the Roman Church. "How can we explain this second century *Drang nach Rom?*" Jalland asks, and he adds, "May there not have been a conviction, common to Justin, Valentinus, Marcion and the others, that in some way or another, the Roman See had an inherent right to pronounce an opinion on their doctrine, and moreover that the nature of its decision, i.e., whether favorable or adverse, would seriously affect their prospects of success in obtaining for their teaching general acceptance by the Church at large?" [18]

Tertullian

Tertullian, while still a Catholic, occasionally bore witness to the authority which the Roman Church enjoyed because of its apostolic origin. Thus in his *De Praescriptione haereticorum,* written in 200, he speaks of the registers in which the churches keep the roll of their bishops, and in particular that of "the Church of Rome, which makes Clement to have been ordained in like manner by Peter.... You have Rome from which comes into our hands the very authority [of the Apostles themselves]. How happy is its church, on which the Apostles poured forth all their doctrine along with their blood! Where Peter endures a passion like his Lord's! Where Paul wins his crown in a death like John's!..." [19]

After Tertullian left the Church in 211 to join the Montanist sect, he was very critical of Pope St. Callistus, whom he accused of laxism in his treatment of penitents. "The sovereign pontiff and bishop of bishops," he wrote, "issued an edict, and this in peremptory fashion...." [20] It is likely that these terms were used by Catholics to designate the Bishop of Rome. However that may be, Pope Callistus by his decree put an end to the rigorism which Tertullian was defending.

St. Cyprian

St. Cyprian, the Bishop of Carthage, who suffered martyrdom in 258, bore witness to the primacy of the Roman Church in his book *De Unitate Ecclesiae.* This

Church, he wrote, is the source of unity for the whole Catholic world because it is the See of Peter, just as the Church of Carthage, on account of its antiquity, is the source of unity for the churches of Roman Africa.

Cyprian later disagreed with Pope St. Stephen on the question of rebaptizing heretics who were converted to the Church, and he has been made out to be an adversary of the Roman primacy and a champion of episcopal independence. Dom John Chapman, who became a Catholic as the result of his study of the case of Cyprian, held that Cyprian is a witness to the primacy of Rome, but was not as logical as he might have been, perhaps because he was made a bishop just a few years after his conversion to the Christian faith.

The fact is that within a short time the whole Church, including the churches of Africa, had adopted the Roman rule of not rebaptizing converts from heresy who had been validly baptized.

In 261, Pope St. Denis set out the Catholic faith with authority, defending the orthodoxy of Denis, Bishop of Alexandria, who had been accused of heresy. Both Denis of Alexandria and his accusers took it as proper that the case should be referred to Rome for judgment, and were ready to abide by the Pope's decision.

From this brief account of the evidence available concerning the 2nd and 3rd centuries, it is clear that the authority of Rome as the See of Peter was recognized in the East and West, that is, by the whole Church.

In the frequent disputes that arose after the promulgation of the *Edict of Toleration* in 312, the primacy of the Roman Pontiff was so understood that communion with him was regarded by all the bishops of the world as the necessary condition and sufficient sign of orthodoxy and full communion with the Church.

This was the case, whether it was a question of schism, as with the Donatists in Africa, or of heresy, as with the Arians, Pelagians and Nestorians. In each dispute, the opposing parties strove to have the Roman Pontiff on their side. The orthodox faith was determined, not by the number of bishops favoring a certain view, but by the Roman Pontiff. Catholics were preserved and confirmed in their orthodoxy by communion with Rome.

Heretics, before they were condemned, sought the approval of Rome, and when they were condemned, it was Rome that they attacked. Universal jurisdiction was not only exercised, but also claimed by the Roman Pontiffs. Had it been an innovation, there would have been protests; but the Roman claims were not contested.

How Did the See of Rome Acquire This Primacy?

As we have seen, Christ appointed Peter to be the chief shepherd of His flock, and Peter was recognized as head of the Church during the early years of her existence.

Peter's Function as Rock

When Christ promised Peter the primacy, He made it clear that He intended to make him the rock on which the Church was to be built, that is, the source of its unity and stability.

Was it in the mind of Christ that Peter should have successors in his office as head of the Church? Oscar Cullmann thinks not. For him, Peter's role is unique, and not transmissible to successors. Cullmann is a Protestant, and this view is consistent with his Protestant theology.

Ethelbert Stauffer, on the other hand, refuses to rule out the possibility that Christ intended Peter to have successors. He writes: "Did Jesus Himself think of a successor to Peter? The idea is not impossible, for the notion of succession was widespread in the realm of biblical practice. God was Israel's heavenly shepherd, though Moses was His representative on earth, and after Moses' death the shepherd's staff was passed on from hand to hand throughout the generations. The mediatorial office which Moses received from God's hand was quite unique. Nevertheless, he appointed Joshua to be his successor, and the historical uniqueness of Moses remained unaffected. But it was essential to have a successor in office who could ascend his *cathedra*. Consequently the raised chair on which the Ruler of the Synagogue sits is known as *Cathedra Mosis*. Moses received the law from heaven, and handed it on to a long succession of bearers of the tradition that has persisted right down to our own times. Thoughts such as these were much alive and active in the time of Jesus. But Jesus did count on Peter dying before the history of the Church and of the world attained its goal (Jn. 21:18). Should Peter also have a successor? The uniqueness of Peter's position in the history of the Church is not affected thereby. He is the rock, and he alone. Must not someone take over his office, the shepherd's staff and the keys? (cf. Is. 22:22) Perhaps Jesus had already talked about such future eventualities (Jn. 21:22)."[21]

If we grant that Christ intended to establish a Church and foresaw that its unity and stability would be threatened, we can hardly deny that He would have foreseen the need for someone who would fulfill the role that originally pertained to Peter.

It is a historical fact that the only person in the history of the Church who has fulfilled this role is the Bishop of Rome, whom Christians through the ages have acknowledged as Head of the Church because he is the successor of St. Peter.

Peter Was Bishop in Rome

It is certain that Peter came to Rome and suffered martyrdom there in the persecution of Nero that broke out in 65. The contention of some early Protestant propagandists that Peter never came to Rome is now quite discredited, for the historical evidence to the contrary is overwhelming. There is the reference to "Babylon" in 1 Peter 5:13; the testimony of Clement in his Letter to the Corinthians 5-6; that of Ignatius in his Letter to the Romans; the assertion of Papias that St. Mark wrote his Gospel while Peter was preaching in Rome, etc. His tomb has been venerated there from the earliest times and no other city has ever claimed that he was buried there.[22]

That Peter governed the Church of Rome during his last sojourn there may be taken for granted. As the chief of the Apostles he was much more than a bishop. Those who succeeded him were bishops of Rome. St. Irenaeus, writing in 180, tells us who they were: "When therefore the blessed Apostles [i.e., Peter and Paul] had laid the foundations and erected the church [i.e., of Rome], they entrusted the liturgical office of the episcopate to Linus. And Cletus succeeded him, after whom Clement is ordained to the episcopate in the third place [in the series] from the Apostles. Yet though he actually saw the Apostles and conversed with them, and afterward had the teaching of the Apostles ringing in his ears and their *paradosis* [i.e., teaching] in sight, he was not the only one; for many were still surviving at that time who had been instructed by the Apostles.... And Evaristus succeeds this Clement; and Alexander, Evaristus; then in the same manner Sixtus is made the sixth after the Apostles, and after him Telesphorus, who also bore noble witness. Afterward Hyginus, then Pius, after whom was Anicetus. When Soter had succeeded Anicetus, now Eleutherius possesses the order of episcopate in the twelfth place from the Apostles...." [23]

This list is important, even though Irenaeus was mainly concerned to establish that the doctrine taught by the Apostles had been handed down by an unbroken continuity of teachers in the See of Rome.

Bishops Inherit the Prerogatives of Their Predecessors

That bishops should inherit the prerogatives of their predecessors is asserted by St. Clement in his Letter to the Corinthians. He declares moreover that this principle is of apostolic origin. He writes: "Similarly, our Apostles knew, through our Lord Jesus Christ that there would be dissensions over the title of bishop. In their full foreknowledge of this, therefore, they proceeded to appoint the ministers I spoke of, and they went on to add the instruction that if these should fall asleep, other accredited persons should succeed them in their office." [24]

That the bishops of Rome succeeded Peter not only in his headship of the Roman Church but also in his primacy over the whole Church is a historical fact. As we have seen, the Roman Pontiffs exercised this primacy from the beginning and their right to do so was not challenged until the 11th Century. All agreed that the primacy which Christ conferred on Peter was intended by Him as a permanent feature of His Church, and was the prerogative of his successors in the See of Rome. St. Thomas More, it may be remembered, at first thought the Roman primacy was of ecclesiastical origin, but after diligent inquiry came to the conclusion that its origin is divine. And this, since the First Vatican Council, is the official teaching of the Catholic Church: "If anyone denies that in virtue of the decree of Our Lord Christ Himself [i.e., by divine institution] Blessed Peter has perpetual successors in his Primacy over the Universal Church, let him be anathema." [25]

The Origin of the Roman Primacy

Some have argued that the Roman Primacy owes its origin to the fact that it was because Rome was the capital of the Empire that the bishop of that See is recognized as Head of the Church.

The fact is that the bishops throughout the world acknowledge the primacy of the Bishop of Rome because he is the successor of St. Peter. It is in fact quite absurd to suppose that it was respect for the imperial capital that led the Christians of the early centuries to recognize the primacy of the Roman See.

"What Christians of the period really thought about the *city* of Rome," Jalland writes, "may be judged by the uncomplimentary allusions to it in the Apocalypse, or from Tatian's sardonic reference to 'Roman arrogance.' And in the face of expressions used by those who, like Tertullian, were eager to satirize the methods by which she rose to power, or, following the example of Hippolytus, denounced the whole ordered majesty of Roman rule as a diabolical parody of the kingdom of God, can we seriously suppose that the respect paid by Christians like Ignatius to the Roman Church is explicable solely by the view that it arose from the association of that church in their minds with the center of Roman government? Surely it would be much nearer the truth to say that it was honored not because of but in spite of the imperial associations. In view of the evident abhorrence of secular Rome felt by 2nd Century Christians, it must be supposed that they had an overwhelmingly strong reason for honoring its church which no mere worldly prepotency can be sufficient to explain." [26]

The Roman Primacy as the Guarantee of Unity

It is a well-established historical fact that without the Roman primacy there can be no unity in faith or government.

The Eastern Orthodox are split into a score of national churches, and the Protestants into innumerable sects.

The Roman primacy is also the guarantee of independence for the local Church *vis-à-vis* the state.

Among the schismatic Orthodox the government of the Church has often been in the hands of laymen. So it was in Russia under Peter the Great and Catherine the Great.

In Constantinople the Patriarch was subject to the Sultan of Turkey and on his orders excommunicated the bishops of Greece when Greece became independent in 1833. The same year, the Greek Church became the established Church of the country on the authority of King Otto.

The Lutheran churches of Germany and Scandinavia were from the beginning under lay control. The Anglican Church was established by the civil authority in the 16th Century and it still accepts the principle of royal supremacy, its bishops being appointed by the Crown.

The kings of France and Spain and the Emperor endeavored to bring the Church in their dominions entirely under their control, but they never quite succeeded, for the national church was only a part of the wider Church, of which the Pope was the head.

With acceptance of the Roman primacy, the unity of Christians is secured. Where it is rejected, disintegration into a multitude of ecclesiastical bodies inevitably follows. The Rock on which Christ built His Church is her guarantee of stability and unity, and there is no other.

Notes

1. *New Testament Theology* (tr. John March), SCM Press, London, 1955, pp. 31-32.

2. *Ibid.,* pp. 32-33.

3. C. S. Lewis has remarked that Bultmann was mistaken in holding that St. Matthew has put things back to front, for "logically, emotionally and imaginatively, the sequence is perfect." *Christian Reflections*, Geoffrey Bles, London, 1967, p. 156.

4. No. 100; PG 6:709c.

5. Bk. III, ch. 24, no. 3; PG 7:967a.

6. In Ante-Nicene Library, Edinburgh, 1897, Section XXIII, no. 37.

7. No. 22, PL 2:34.

8. *Peter: Disciple—Apostle—Martyr,* SCM Press, London, 1953, p. 185.

9. *The Church and the Papacy,* SPCK, London, 1944, p. 98.

10. *Summa Theologiae,* II-II. q. 33, a. 4, ad 2um.

11. Epistula no. 65, PL 54:879.

12. Cited by D'Herbigny, *De Ecclesia,* Beauchesne, Paris, 1928, Vol. II, p. 177.

13. Edmundson, in his book *The Church in Rome in the First Century,* Longmans, Green, London, 1913, pp. 45-46, comments on this and quotes A. Peter, remarking that nothing remains of the work of thirty-five historical writers who flourished between 37 and 138.

14. Edmundson dates the *Epistle of Clement* in 70, and John A. T. Robinson accepts this dating as probable. *Redating the New Testament,* pp. 328-335.

15. *First Epistle of Clement,* no. 48, no. 59, in *Early Christian Writings,* pp. 48-49, 54.

16. Book III, ch. 3, no. 2 (tr. A. Roberts, and W. H. Rambaut), Edinburgh, 1884.

17. Jalland, *The Church and the Papacy,* p. 121.

18. *Ibid.,* p. 109.

19. Ch. 32 and ch. 36, PL 2:45 and 49.

20. *De Pudicitia,* ch. 1; PL 2:981.

21. *New Testament Theology,* p. 33.

22. Edmundson in his book *The Church in Rome in the First Century* maintains that there is very strong *prima facie* case for the view that the Church was founded in Rome by St. Peter, who would have come there in the early 40's. Cf. p. 59.
23. *Adversus Haereses,* bk. 3, ch. 3, no. 3.
24. No. 44.
25. Session IV, ch. 2, canon 1; Denzinger *Enchiridion Symbolorum,* ed. 18-20, no. 1825.
26. *The Church and the Papacy,* pp. 105-106.

References

S. Jaki, *And on This Rock,* Ave Maria Press, Notre Dame, Indiana, 1978. A modern Catholic scholar comments on Matthew 16:18, and puts the saying in its geographical background.

Oscar Cullmann, *Peter: Disciple—Apostle—Martyr,* (tr. Floyd V. Filson), SCM Press, London, 1953. This book is presented by the author, a famous Reformed theologian, as a historical study concerning the Apostle Peter.

T. G. Jalland, *The Church and the Papacy: A Historical Study* (The Bampton Lectures for 1942), SPCK, London, 1944. An Anglican Scholar studies the evidence for the primacy of Peter and finds it convincing.

G. Edmundson, *The Church in Rome in the First Century* (The Bampton Lectures for 1913), Longmans, Green, London, 1913. Edmundson, as John A. T. Robinson has noted, throws a great deal of light on the Roman Church and on Peter in particular.

A. Harnack, *The History of Dogma* (tr. Neil Buchanan), Williams and Norgate, London, 1896. Harnack's *excursus* "Catholic and Roman," Vol. II, pp. 149-168, is especially informative.

Epilogue

We have considered only some of the evidence which shows that the Catholic religion is the work of God. Much more could have been brought forward in support of our case. Thus, we have not discussed how Christ fulfilled the prophecies of the Old Testament concerning the Messiah, nor have we dealt with the fruitfulness of the Church as she has gone about doing good while persevering in her primary task of helping men to save their immortal souls— and this in bad times as in good, while she was enduring persecution or was favored by the state.

If one has accepted that Christ is the Son of God and the Author of a unique divine revelation, one is dispensed in one's quest for the truth from a detailed study of such religions as Buddhism, Confucianism, Taoism and Islam, which are of merely human origin.

The truth that the Catholic Church is the work of God cannot be demonstrated by rational argument, for it is known with certainty only by the light of faith. But it can be shown that the divine origin of the Church is beyond reasonable doubt.

Doubt is always possible about what is not so directly evident as the existence of the visible universe—and there have been thinkers who have held that even this can be doubted—so that men *can* doubt whether there is a future life, or whether God exists, or Christ worked the miracles recorded in the Gospels. But whether such doubt is reasonable is another matter, and the tenor of our argument has been that it is not.

For the assent of faith, which excludes all doubt, we need a supernatural illumination, which is the work of divine grace. This assent, therefore, transcends reason. But it does not do violence to reason, and it is the function of apologetical argument such as has engaged our attention in these pages to show that this is indeed the case—that in assenting to the mysteries that are at the heart of our religion as revealed by God, we are assenting to what is beyond the range of reason, but also beyond reasonable doubt.

Daughters of St. Paul

ALASKA
750 West 5th Ave., Anchorage, AK 99501 **907-272-8183.**
CALIFORNIA
3335 Motor Ave., W. Los Angeles, CA 90034 **213-202-8144.**
1570 Fifth Ave. (at Cedar Street), San Diego, CA 92101 **619-232-1442.**
46 Geary Street, San Francisco, CA 94108 **415-781-5180.**
CONNECTICUT
Bridgeport: Please check your phone book for current listing.
FLORIDA
2700 Biscayne Blvd., Miami, FL 33137 **305-573-1618.**
HAWAII
1143 Bishop Street, Honolulu, HI 96813 **808-521-2731.**
ILLINOIS
172 North Michigan Ave., Chicago, IL 60601 **312-346-4228; 312-346-3240.**
LOUISIANA
423 Main Street, Baton Rouge, LA 70802 **504-343-4057; 504-336-1504.**
4403 Veterans Blvd., Metairie, LA 70006 **504-887-7631; 504-887-0113.**
MASSACHUSETTS
50 St. Paul's Ave., Jamaica Plain, Boston, MA 02130 **617-522-8911.**
Rte. 1, 450 Providence Hwy., Dedham, MA 02026 **617-326-5385.**
MISSOURI
1001 Pine Street (at North 10th), St. Louis, MO 63101 **314-621-0346.**
NEW JERSEY
Hudson Mall, Route 440 and Communipaw Ave.,
    Jersey City, NJ 07304 **201-433-7740.**
NEW YORK
625 East 187th Street, Bronx, NY 10458 **212-584-0440.**
59 East 43rd Street, New York, NY 10017 **212-986-7580.**
78 Fort Place, Staten Island, NY 10301 **718-447-5071; 718-447-5086.**
OHIO
616 Walnut Street, Cincinnati, OH 45202 **513-421-5733.**
2105 Ontario Street (at Prospect Ave.), Cleveland, OH 44115
    216-621-9427.
PENNSYLVANIA
1719 Chestnut Street, Philadelphia, PA 19103 **215-568-2638;
    215-864-0991.**
SOUTH CAROLINA
243 King Street, Charleston, SC 29401 **803-577-0175.**
TEXAS
114 Main Plaza, San Antonio, TX 78205 **512-224-8101.**
VIRGINIA
1025 King Street, Alexandria, VA 22314 **703-549-3806.**
WASHINGTON
2301 Second Ave. (at Bell), Seattle, WA 98121 **206-441-4100.**
CANADA
3022 Dufferin Street, Toronto 395, Ontario, Canada.